ORGANIZATIONAL CULTURE IN THE MANAGEMENT OF MERGERS

ORGANIZATIONAL CULTURE IN THE MANAGEMENT OF MERGERS

Afsaneh Nahavandi
and
Ali R. Malekzadeh

Q

Quorum Books
WESTPORT, CONNECTICUT • LONDON

658.16
N15o

Library of Congress Cataloging-in-Publication Data

Nahavandi, Afsaneh.
   Organizational culture in the management of mergers / Afsaneh
Nahavandi and Ali R. Malekzadeh.
      p.   cm.
   Includes bibliographical references (p.   ) and index.
   ISBN 0–89930–669–1 (alk. paper)
   1. Organizational change—Management.   2. Consolidation and merger
of corporations—Management.   3. Corporate reorganizations—
Management.   4. Consolidation and merger of corporations—
Management—Case studies.   5. Corporate reorganizations—
Management—Case studies.   I. Malekzadeh, Ali R.   II. Title.
HD58.8.N34   1993
658.1′6—dc20   92–44685

British Library Cataloguing in Publication Data is available.

Library of Congress Catalog Card Number: 92–44685
ISBN: 0–89930–669–1

First published in 1993

Quorum Books, 88 Post Road West, Westport, CT 06881
An imprint of Greenwood Publishing Group, Inc.

Printed in the United States of America

The paper used in this book complies with the
Permanent Paper Standard issued by the National
Information Standards Organization (Z39.48–1984).

10 9 8 7 6 5 4 3 2 1

To our parents,
who gave us the love of learning

Contents

Preface

The purpose of this book is twofold: (1) to demonstrate the importance of organizational culture and people in the successful management of mergers and (2) to provide a framework for analyzing and managing the process of merging cultures, people, and strategies. We hope to provide the reader with information that can be used in planning the merger of two organizations.

Although much has been written about mergers, the central focus has been on the financial aspects. We first became interested in mergers about ten years ago when one of us attended a conference at which John Berry, an eminent cross-cultural psychologist, presented his research showing how the native cultures of Canada have adapted to pressures from the dominant Canadian culture. Berry had no interest in organizational mergers, but his ideas appeared to be so pertinent to mergers that, after the conference, we began the process of researching the role of culture in merger strategies and eventually developed the model that became the foundation for this book.

WHO SHOULD READ THIS BOOK

This book is targeted to all individuals who, as members of acquiring or acquired organizations, have the power to negotiate some of the processes for the implementation of mergers, as well as to those who are simply at the receiving end of all the changes. Executives who negotiate a merger can use the ideas presented in this book to plan for the cultural aspects that are often the key to the success of a merger. Less influential bystanders can also gain an understanding of the cultural adaptation processes that

underlie a merger and perhaps find some solace in being provided with
labels to describe what is happening to their organization.

This book should also be of interest to students and scholars who have
interest in mergers, since it provides a number of theories and examples
of the success and failure of mergers. While we have tried to avoid academic
jargon as much as possible, we have also shied away from oversimplifying
the concepts. Mergers are highly complex events; it would be a disservice
to all those who negotiate, plan, and live through them to ignore those
complexities.

ORGANIZATION AND CONTENTS

Part I (Chapters 2 through 4) lays the foundation for understanding
mergers from a strategic and cultural point of view. In each of these three
chapters, one aspect of organizations is presented. Chapter 2 defines the
concept of organizational culture. The role of the leader in the creation of
culture is also discussed, along with the functions of culture within an
organization. Specifically, attention is given to the role of culture in helping
to maintain organizational health and external adaptability. The topics of
cultural strength as well as cultural change are discussed as precursors to
the topic of acculturation.

Chapter 3 focuses on mergers as corporate strategy. It describes the four
major types of mergers: related, concentric, vertical, and conglomerate.
Each is discussed in terms of the bargaining power it affords an organization, the degree to which resources have to be exchanged, the level of
personnel interaction involved, the time required for implementation, the
potential for profitability, and the risk involved. Each of these concepts is
used in subsequent chapters to provide an understanding of the processes
involved in merging two organizations. Chapter 4 focuses on the challenges
inherent in merging the structures of two organizations. The chapter presents the elements and determinants of structure and then discusses the
way in which each type of merger affects them.

Part II focuses on the concept of acculturation and the role of leaders
in the formulation and implementation of mergers. Specifically, Chapter
5 provides a detailed description of the concept of acculturation. The factors
that determine the course of acculturation for the two merging partners
are identified and described. The roles of organizational culture, strategy,
and structure in the acculturation process are also clarified. Chapter 6
focuses on the special role leaders play in the merger process and in determining the course of acculturation.

And finally, Part III presents four case studies. Each of the cases is a
composite of the types of mergers we have encountered over the years.
Although the cases are fictitious, key elements within them are very real,
as they have been borrowed from real mergers. Each case represents a

particular type of merger and one of the modes of acculturation described in Chapter 5. The concepts of organizational culture, strategy, structure, and leadership are interwoven in each case to provide a practical example of each mode. An analysis is presented at the end of each case along with a list of factors that need to be addressed to manage each mode of acculturation successfully.

Chapter 7 presents a case involving the merger between two airlines and the challenges the merger partners face in trying to create one organization out of two related ones. The culture, strategy, and leadership of the two partners lend themselves to complete assimilation of one into the other. Chapter 8 describes a merger between two computer firms, each firm from a different market. In this case, the mode of acculturation is integration as required by the culture, strategy, and leadership of the two firms. An example of separation is provided in Chapter 9 with the conglomerate merger of a biotechnology firm with an industrial control device company.

The last case provided is an example of a failed merger. The scenario in Chapter 10 is unfortunately too familiar: Lack of concern for cultural factors and a heavy-handed approach by the acquiring firm lead to cultural disintegration and the destruction of the firm it had acquired and result in a failure to achieve the goals of the merger. The case is followed by specific pointers on how such a situation can be avoided.

The book ends with a summary of the factors affecting the cultural aspects of mergers and a look at the future of mergers in light of the demographic and economic predictions for the next century.

Acknowledgments

Many people helped us to develop the ideas for this book. Our model of acculturation in mergers was greatly influenced by John Berry. As the individual who developed the concept of the modes of acculturation, he has had an indelible effect on our work through his research and writings. Many of our colleagues have also influenced our thinking: Mike Lubatkin, Dave Jemison, Phil Mirvis, Mitchell Marks, Harbir Singh, Dave Schweiger, Gordon Walter, Hugh O'Neil, Sayan Chattergee, Tony Buono, and Jim Bowditch, to name a few. We would also like to acknowledge Marty Chemers and Irv Altman for providing us with a broad worldview that encouraged the integration of ideas and thoughts.

Additionally, we would like to express our gratitude to our many friends and colleagues at Arizona State University West for their support and patience while we focused our attention on the writing of this book. Finally, we thank our two daughters, Parisa and Arianne, who had to put up with Mom and Dad working many weekends and late nights.

ORGANIZATIONAL CULTURE IN THE MANAGEMENT OF MERGERS

1

Introduction: The Forgotten Side of Mergers

In the 1970s and 1980s, thousands of firms were bought and sold, and the period has been characterized by many as an era of "merger mania." Now that the trend has waned, we are just beginning to learn the outcome of many of the mergers that occurred during those hectic decades. Some of these mergers and takeovers were made primarily with a short-term goal of profit making based on the dismantling and selling of a firm's assets. Others were undertaken based on a variety of strategic motives. Some firms selected a merger over the internal development of a new product or service. Others felt a need to increase their market share, and a merger with a competitor seemed the easiest way to become more competitive in the firm's industry. Still other firms diversified into new industries in order to avoid the cyclical downturns of a single industry.

Regardless of the goals, the mergers that have taken place in the past few years have been a major cause of the tremendous restructuring that has now become a reality in a majority of U.S. companies. As companies were bought and sold, attempts were made at reaching synergy, which often meant cutting duplicating departments, combining related areas, and overall becoming leaner.

TYPICAL FOCUS OF BUSINESS PUBLICATIONS REGARDING MERGERS

In preparation for this book, we undertook a broad review of the literature in search of examples to add to our existing list. We found a plethora of information about mergers, the majority of which have been dissected and critiqued thoroughly. Much has been written about whether the purchase price was reasonable and which new markets will be open to the parent firm. Proxy fights are detailed. Stock prices are discussed at length, channels of distribution are mentioned, and financial benefits to consumers are predicted. Furthermore, much of the research provides detailed recommendations on planning a merger by focusing on pricing methods and providing negotiation advice.

A review of the literature confirmed many of our suspicions as well. In all these discussions, the impressive amount of financial and operational information is accompanied by limited information about the organizational and cultural aspects of mergers. Employees and managers are only mentioned in passing. Occasionally, we came across statistics about manager layoffs. The general topic of industry restructuring and its effect on the economy is discussed but often with limited consideration of the effect such restructuring has on the people it affects most directly—namely, the employees of the targeted firms. There is very little mention of what happens to the people who get "restructured" and even less mention of what happens to the culture of these organizations. Once in a while, we found a passing mention of "resistance." However, even then, the descriptions are often superficial. For example, dress code and communication style differences are discussed, or one firm's "stuffy" and the other's "relaxed" management styles are mentioned. Some examples of how employees refuse to use the new logo or how the old badges don't get turned in may be provided, but discussions rarely go beyond this point.

WHY DO MERGERS FAIL?

It is very difficult to estimate how many of the mergers and acquisitions of the 1980s have succeeded. It is even more difficult to define what *success* means. Some estimate, however, that close to 80 percent of mergers do not meet their premerger financial goals and that almost 50 percent are failures.[1] The common measure of stock market reactions one day—or even a few months—after the merger is undoubtedly inadequate. In spite of theories that the stock market, in evaluating and valuing a merger, takes into account all the managerial and human factors, they clearly do not reflect the human and cultural costs of mergers—particularly in light of the fact that the managers and leaders involved in a merger often voice their inability to predict its exact outcome. So it is unrealistic to expect that financial markets, having only partial information, be able to make accurate predictions about the outcome of a merger.

However, when reasons for lack of success of a merger are discussed, the focus is still on the financial and strategic issues: "The target firm was overpriced." "There was too much debt." "The parent company should have 'stuck to its knitting.' " "The target firm did not perform up to financial expectations." Once again, the cultural and people aspects of merger are typically ignored. It is rare to see business journalists or chief executive officers (CEOs) admit that the merger's inability to live up to expectations is related, at least partly, to lack of cultural understanding or to failure to consider cultural factors.

It is essential, however, to consider cultural and human factors as part of the definition of success of a merger. How much turnover resulted from the merger? How many managers and employees left the firm? How many years of experience were lost? Is it possible to replace those individuals? What are the costs of replacement? Can the target firm be expected to perform well without those who have left? The turnover of a large group of employees after a merger may have an immediate positive effect on financial statements, since labor costs are reduced. In the long run, however, the loss of many individuals contributes to the lack of success of a merger.

The influence of culture on organizations is difficult to measure and predict. During a merger, that influence becomes even harder to control, since there is much resentment and resistance and since the culture of one organization is not always known to the other party. Guaranteeing managers and employees their jobs is not enough to win them over. Individuals often hang on to seemingly insignificant things: The letterhead of the old company is kept for many years. Name tags with the old logo are not discarded. Employees refuse to use the new name in private conversations. All these events represent resistance to giving up the culture of their company. That culture represents the shared values and norms of the employees. It is what makes the company unique, the glue that bonds people together. Giving it up is equivalent to surrendering one's identity, and consequently, employees often fight to preserve it.

In spite of the power of organizational culture, a majority of acquirers simply expect their new acquisition to relinquish its culture and become part of them. Lack of concern for cultural factors becomes a major obstacle to the success of the merger.

THE ACCULTURATION MODEL

The ideas presented in this book provide a framework for understanding the cultural processes in mergers. Through understanding these factors, managers can make plans for cultural adaptation as an integral part of the premerger negotiations and the postmerger implementation process. The model presented in Figure 1.1 introduces the major concepts that will be used throughout the book.

At the heart of our model is the concept of *acculturation*. The term has been borrowed from anthropology and cross-cultural psychology and refers to the process by which two or more cultures come in contact and resolve the conflict that arises as a result of this contact. As will be discussed at

Figure 1.1
Determinant Factors of Acculturation in Mergers

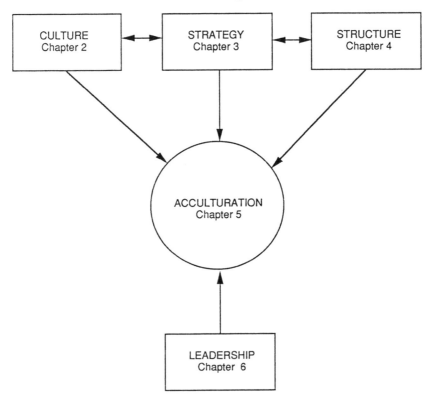

length in Chapter 5, acculturation takes place in stages and can take a number of different forms. The point is, however, that when two organizations come in contact during a merger, their cultures will undergo a number of changes or will resist making changes. To prevent resistance, those changes have to be carefully negotiated and mapped out.

Factors in Acculturation

Culture. The culture of an organization consists of the elements that make an organization unique. Culture is to an organization what personality is to an individual. Culture is what makes an organization unique and holds the members of an organization together. The cultures of the two merging partners—particularly their strength and the level to which each tolerates diversity—constitute one of the main determinants of the course of acculturation. If an acquired organization has a strong culture that is highly valued by its members, it is likely to resist the efforts of an acquirer to impose its own culture and managerial practices. The way an acquirer deals with its acquisitions is also partly determined by its culture. As a result, understanding organizational culture is an indispensable part of successful merger implementation.

Strategy. The strategy of an organization involves how it plans to achieve its mission and goals and is partly determined by its culture. However, strategy can also become one of the factors that influence the evolution of culture. Therefore, it is very difficult to disconnect the two elements. In the case of mergers, strategy focuses mainly on the goal and the type of merger intended. In particular, the goal of the merger is one of the defining factors of the course of acculturation. How much the two firms will have to be integrated will determine how much contact is required between the two firms.

Structure. The structure of an organization refers to the way in which its human resources are organized. As is the case with strategy, structure both determines and is determined by culture. Furthermore, strategy and structure are closely linked and influence one another. As one of the major representations of culture, the understanding and proper management of structure during a merger constitute a vital factor in acculturation.

Leadership. The last factor presented in Figure 1.1 is leadership. Given that leadership becomes particularly important in times of crisis, such as during mergers, it is crucial to understand the role and influence of leaders in the acculturation process. Leaders with different styles may have different preferences for merger strategies and merger implementation.

Other Factors. There are probably a number of other factors that influence the course of acculturation. For example, one needs to look at employee personalities and consider how different types of people are likely to react to a merger. Economic and political factors also play a role, as they undoubtedly did during the 1980s' merger mania.

While these other factors are important, we chose to focus our analysis on culture, strategy, and structure because they provide the foundation for understanding the acculturation process and because they can be managed and influenced by managers (or leaders).

Overall, the culture, strategy, and structure of a firm are the major factors influencing the type of acculturation that will take place, while leadership plays a key role in the way in which the acculturation is implemented.

WHY DO WE NEED TO FOCUS ON ACCULTURATION?

While the frequency of mergers has decreased, they remain one of the most popular growth strategies for many businesses. The lack of success of so many of the best-intentioned mergers indicates that there is a gap in our understanding of what needs to be done to make mergers work. Research investigating the human costs of mergers[2] indicates that culture and the proper management of cultural factors during a merger may provide a key to the problem. The model and ideas presented in this book provide a framework that allows for understanding the events and processes that occur during the various stages of a merger. Through understanding the merger process, executives and managers will be better equipped to handle cultural issues and thereby ease the transition.

NOTES

1. *Personnel Administrator*, August 1989, pp. 84–90.

2. For an analysis of the human costs of mergers see A. F. Buono & J. L. Bowditch, *The human side of mergers and acquisition* (San Francisco: Jossey-Bass, 1989).

Part I

The Foundations

2

Culture in Mergers

Management scholars and practitioners have found the focus on the financial and rational aspects of organizations to lack explanatory power. We cannot understand organizations by considering only their formal, rational, and objective sides. Many unstated rules, norms, and assumptions that influence behavior and decision making are not reflected in formal organizational charts, job descriptions, and financial statements. As a result, the concept of organizational culture has been used to explore that softer, less measurable aspect of organization. It has become a given that organizations have distinct cultures in much the same way that individuals have distinct personalities. The culture of an organization—just like the personality of an individual—gives it a unique identity that leads it to behave in particular ways. Just as with personality, culture is difficult to measure and in constant development.

This chapter will define organizational culture and discuss the role of leaders in its formation. The functions of culture and the advantages and disadvantages of strong cultures in organizational change will also be examined.

WHAT IS ORGANIZATIONAL CULTURE?

The *Webster's New Collegiate Dictionary* (1980) defines *culture* as "the integrated pattern of human behavior that includes thought, speech, action, and artifacts and depends on man's capacity for learning and transmitting knowledge to succeeding generations" and "the customary beliefs, social forms, and material traits of a racial, religious, or social group." These definitions point to several important aspects of culture. First, culture permeates all human behaviors and interactions. Second, culture is shared by members of a group. And third, it is handed down to newcomers and from one generation to the next. This definition of culture is not aimed at organizations but is very applicable to them.

As is the case with social or racial groups, organizations develop certain assumptions, norms, and patterns of speech and behavior that make them unique. Also, similar to social or racial groups, culture is one of the factors that differentiates one organization from another. Applying the concept of culture to organizations gives them a human quality. Organizations become much more than the profit margin, the buildings, and the organizational charts. As living entities, organizations grow and change. They adapt to their environment and maintain internal health.

Many management scholars have focused on the concept of organizational culture.[1] It is generally defined as a series of basic assumptions that an organization has developed in learning to cope with its external environment and its internal functioning. These assumptions have been found to be effective and valid and are therefore communicated to new employees.[2] Culture makes each organization unique and bonds members of an organization together. The culture of the organization determines what behaviors and ideas are acceptable and appropriate.

Culture is the yardstick used to evaluate many behaviors and ideas, and it provides a basis for the development of goals and strategies. For example, an organization where one of the basic assumptions is that people perform best under minimal control and supervision and need autonomy to excel would consider heavy-handed management techniques used by one of their new managers unacceptable. Furthermore, such an organization would be more likely to select a training program for developing participative management skills over one focusing on methods for developing power. A case in point is the much-publicized W. L. Gore and Associates, with headquarters in Newark, Delaware, that makes wire and cable, medical products, Gore-tex fibers and fabrics, and industrial filter bags. One of the distinguishing characteristics of the firm is its informality and the absence of hierarchy and status symbols. Employees and managers do not have formal titles, and creative problem solving is highly encouraged. As a result, the use of status symbols that would indicate a hierarchy are considered highly inappropriate. This example demonstrates how a basic cultural assumption about factors that lead to effectiveness is used to determine which behaviors are acceptable.

Levels of Culture

A very useful and practical way of analyzing organizational culture is to divide it into three levels.[3]

Level One: Artifacts. The first level of culture is composed of the visible artifacts and behaviors within an organization. It includes the architecture and design of the building in which the organization is housed, the office layout, the art objects used, and the dress and demeanor of managers and employees. The various artifacts are carefully constructed by the members of the organization. They are all observable, although not always easily interpretable. They can only be fully understood when considered within the context of the organization's values and basic assumptions. A simple description of the various artifacts of an organization will provide a glimpse of, rather than a thorough understanding of, the culture. The latter can be achieved by considering values and assumptions.

An example of cultural artifacts is office design. Organizations use different designs for their offices. Some are open with no walls or only very short partitions and no clear and specific status symbols. Others have closed offices of different sizes that correspond to occupant status. Office layout alone, however, does not give one much information about the organization. Layout design may reflect the industry or the culture of the organization. As a result, an open office may represent either an open participative culture or a need to monitor employees. In order to understand the significance of the office layout and its implications, one needs to examine the values and assumptions that lie at the deeper levels of culture.

Level Two: Values. The second, deeper level of culture is composed of values held by members of an organization. These values indicate what ought to be and determine what is considered acceptable. For example, an organization may value training and development of employees, considering training to be essential to organizational effectiveness. To value training (level two) would lead to the observable presence and use of training programs (level one).

Some values in the organization are clearly stated and defined; others are more fuzzy and less accessible. Values that are based on common experiences within the organization and have been found to be useful will become an integral part of the organization. These deeply held values are often very good indicators of behavior and decision making. On the other hand, some values are espoused by members of an organization without being fully accepted. As a result, such values do not necessarily predict behaviors.[4] The example of the office layout can be used again to clarify the levels of culture. Open offices in two organizations may stem from different values. In one organization, the open office may result from valuing cooperation, whereas in another organization, the open office is used as a means for close supervision of employees. The same cultural artifact takes on different meaning depending on the value upon which it is based.

Understanding organizational values, in addition to artifacts, provides a deeper and more thorough knowledge of the culture of an organization.

However, values and artifacts may still appear incongruent, and specific patterns may not be discernible. A full understanding of the culture of an organization can only come about with knowledge of the basic underlying assumptions that guide both the development of values and the creation of artifacts. These assumptions constitute the third level of culture.

Level Three: Assumptions. The third level of culture is composed of the basic assumptions resulting from an organization's successes and failures in dealing with its environment. These assumptions make up the organization's basic philosophy and worldview, and they shape the way the environment and all other events are perceived and interpreted. They are the paradigms that guide all decisions and behaviors. Because assumptions are often deep-seated, members of the organization are often unaware of them. For example, a basic assumption could be the nature of people as fundamentally "good" and internally motivated (such as in a Theory Y approach) or fundamentally "bad" and in need of control (Theory X). An organization holding the second assumption would not even consider delegation and autonomy; close supervision is likely to be the norm. In accordance with such an organization's basic assumption about human nature, managers are likely to value hierarchy, tight control, and formal reporting systems. These values in turn are likely to lead to the creation of manuals and monitoring procedures that attempt to control every aspect of employees' behaviors. In the example of an organization with many training programs, the basic guiding assumption may be that people can learn and change. Such an assumption would be at the base of both values and behaviors. If one focused only on the behaviors, their cause would not be clear. Understanding the basic assumptions clarifies the rational for various organizational artifacts and values. Again using the open office example, although the environment may be similar, one open office may have roots in the belief that people are "bad," whereas the other comes from the belief that teamwork is an integral part of performance.

The basic assumptions that determine organizational culture can be related to the industry to which a firm belongs. For example, high-technology firms are more similar to each other than they are to utilities. But even within an industry, there are many differences that are the result of different adaptations to the external environment and to the influence of a number of other factors. For example, although IBM and Apple are two firms in the same industry, they have very different cultures due to the growth stage, size, and leadership of the two organizations. However, both firms share some attributes, such as a strong customer focus. Such a focus is much weaker in other industries, for example in the construction industry.

Furthermore, an organization's basic assumptions are often, but not always, derived from larger cultural and social assumptions. As a result, members of two organizations from two different cultures may have difficulty understanding each other. Their basic assumptions, which are partly derived from the larger social and cultural context in which they function, can provide roadblocks when dealing with other cultures. For example, Japanese organizations, as a result of the country's culture, operate on the basic assumption that groups, rather than individuals, hold primary responsibility for performance. This assumption is reflected in values placed on teamwork and cooperation, which then translate into group rewards and encouragement of team spirit. American companies, on the other hand, are more likely to focus on individual achievement, even when working in teams—an approach consistent with the traditional American values of individualism and competition. As a result, an American manager who holds the basic assumption that individuality and competitiveness are key to success would be puzzled by the Japanese management style until he or she gains insight into the basic assumptions that guide it.

ROLE OF THE LEADER IN SHAPING CULTURE

One of the major factors in the creation and development of culture is the influence of the founders and other leaders on an organization. Leaders, and particularly founders, leave an almost indelible mark on the assumptions passed down from one generation to the next. As a matter of fact, an organization often comes to mirror its founder's personality. If the founder is control oriented and autocratic, the organization will be centralized and managed in a top-down fashion. If the founder is participative and team oriented, the organization will be decentralized and open. The case of Harold Geneen at ITT provides an appropriate illustration: The founder's controversial, combative style permeated the whole organization. On the other hand, Bill Gore's openness and hands-off style led to the creation of the highly unusual lattice structure for his firm.

The leaders make most, if not all, of the decisions regarding the various factors that will shape culture (see Figure 2.1). Most of the factors described below originally resulted from the culture of the organization. However, once they are in place, they in turn influence the culture that contributed to their creation. Trying to decide whether culture comes before the various organizational elements or whether they come first is only relevant in the early stages of the organizational life cycle. Once the organization is created, culture becomes one of the highly interdependent elements that influence decision making and affect performance.

Role Models

The founders and other leaders are role models for organizational members. Stories are told about them, and myths are created about their courage, creativity, and physical prowess. Such stories help perpetuate leaders' influence on their organizations and therefore safeguard the culture. Fur-

Figure 2.1
The Role of the Leader in Influencing Culture

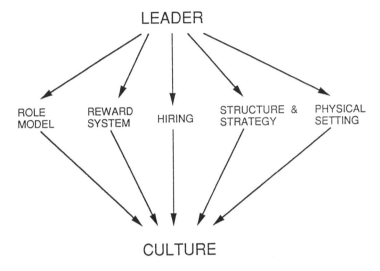

thermore, leaders establish and grant many of the status symbols that are the main artifacts of culture. They grant special awards within the organization that again set up role models for other employees. These role models are more often than not individuals who are excellent representatives of the culture of the organization. For instance, many executives are avid athletes (e.g., John Tees of Dial Corporation). By setting themselves up as role models, they send the signal to their organizations that physical fitness is a key to success.

Reward System

Other means through which the leader shapes culture are by making decisions regarding the reward system and by controlling decision standards. What types of accomplishments will be rewarded is a major aspect of the culture of an organization. The top managers decide which behaviors will be rewarded. In one organization, rewards (both financial and nonfinancial) go only to the highest contributors to the bottom line. In another, other accomplishments such as contributions to cultural diversity and degree of social responsibility are also valued and rewarded. By controlling the reward system, leaders can help maintain or change the culture of their organization.

Hiring Decisions

Top managers are in charge of selecting other top managers. Those selected are likely to fit the existing leader's ideal and therefore fit the culture. The exception is when leaders are brought in specifically to change the organization. In these instances, the new managers are often totally different from the existing managerial culture, and their role is to change the existing culture. Whether to preserve existing culture or to change it, the selection of other influential members of the organization provides leaders with yet another opportunity to shape the culture.

Decisions Regarding Structure and Strategy

The power of the leader to make decisions for the organization regarding structure and strategy is another significant means of shaping culture. By determining the hierarchy, the span of control, the reporting relationship, and the degree of formalization and specialization, the leader molds culture. A highly decentralized and organic structure is likely to be the result of an open and participative culture, whereas a highly centralized structure will go hand in hand with a mechanistic/bureaucratic culture. The structure of an organization limits or encourages interaction and, by doing so, affects, as well as is affected by, the assumptions shared by members of the organization. Similarly, the strategy selected by the leader or the top management team will be determined by, as well as help shape, the culture of the organization. For instance, a proactive differentiation strategy that requires innovation and risk taking will engender a very different culture than a strategy of retrenchment. Similarly, it may be very difficult for an inflexible bureaucracy to implement a highly innovative strategy that requires quick adaptation to the external environment.

Physical Setting

Less direct influence comes from the leader's choice of physical setting. As is the case with other elements discussed, the physical setting is an artifact as well as a generator of culture. The leader's choices regarding the physical setting and building and office design used will establish the patterns of interaction among employees. Such patterns should be designed to reinforce structure and support strategy. For example, if the strategy of the organization hinges on new product development, the structure should encourage cross-functional interaction and teamwork. Such structure is best supported by an open setting that does not present unnecessary barriers to interaction. An open design aimed at increasing interaction is likely to encourage a culture of cooperation and accessibility.

Overall, the leader has many different means of shaping the culture of an organization. Through these various mechanisms and processes, he or she can leave an indelible mark on the organization.

FUNCTIONS OF ORGANIZATIONAL CULTURE

As with any other organizational element, the culture of an organization evolves in order to fulfill a number of functions. If a culture does not satisfy its role, it is likely to be changed or discarded altogether. Culture helps the organization in its two major roles, which are maintaining internal health and defining and adapting to the environment (see Figure 2.2).

Maintaining Internal Health

One of the functions of organizational culture is to help the organization function smoothly by providing the bond that keeps people together. As we will discuss in later sections, the strength of the bond varies from one organization to the next and even within subgroups inside a single organization. However, regardless of the strength, culture provides the identity and collective commitment that are central to encouraging stability in an organization. A healthy culture is essential for the health of the organization.

Giving Identity and Creating Commitment. Culture makes every organization unique. Culture allows one group to set itself apart from others. Therefore, one of the essential aspects of culture is to provide a clear and unique identity to members of an organization. By demonstrating and communicating its culture, an organization can attract and retain employees. The unique identity can also become a source of competitive differentiation in the development of strategy. The presence of an identity leads to higher employee commitment. Belonging to a company with a strong identity provides employees with a sense of family and belonging, which are essential factors in employee morale and satisfaction. Much has been written about the positive aspects of such an identity.

For example, Ben & Jerry's Homemade, Inc.'s informal, socially conscious, and familylike culture has been a source of motivation and success for its employees and managers.[5] Similarly, the benefits of a clear identity have been touted when describing companies such as J. C. Penney, PepsiCo, and UPS.[6] All these companies have unique identities that draw employees together. The closeness instills pride and a sense of ownership in organizational members. The strong identity also fosters commitment to organizational practices. Many organizations, such as UPS, further encourage management commitment by providing stock options.

Another example of culture providing identity and commitment is the Phoenix-based America West, Inc. The company prides itself on being employee oriented and on empowering employees to make decisions. It

Figure 2.2
Functions of Culture

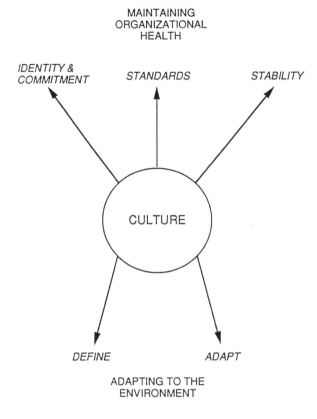

MAINTAINING
ORGANIZATIONAL
HEALTH

*IDENTITY &
COMMITMENT*   *STANDARDS*   *STABILITY*

CULTURE

DEFINE   *ADAPT*

ADAPTING TO THE
ENVIRONMENT

provides twenty-four-hour day care for its employees, requires purchase of stock by all employees, and extensively cross trains them. The culture is highly people oriented and fosters trust and creativity. Many of these characteristics have survived the 1991 Chapter 11 reorganization. America West's culture and resulting organizational practices have led to very strong employee commitment. Even after the Chapter 11 reorganization, many employees expressed total confidence in the company and did not want to leave it. The strong employee commitment that comes from identifying with the company and its culture is one of the essential factors in maintaining internal health.

Providing Standards. Aside from providing a sense of identity and commitment, the culture of an organization also provides the organization with standards for decision making. The basic assumptions of an organization will play a key role in determining what is acceptable with regard to a variety of decisions. What are the parameters for making decisions? How much risk is encouraged or tolerated? Which projects get funded? What is to be used as the basis for rewarding employees and managers? The culture of an organization helps to answer these questions. The level of risk that managers are allowed to take in their decision making is considerably different from one company to another. The basis for evaluation and compensation may also differ. Although the bottom line is an overwhelming concern, many other factors come into play.

For example, US West, Inc. which is often cited as being in the forefront of managing diversity and cultural pluralism, evaluates its managers on how well they have contributed to the company's pluralism goals. The culture of the organization focuses on diversity as a central element, and as a result, diversity becomes part of the evaluation standards. Another example of a company using culture as one of the yardsticks for evaluation and decision making is Johnson & Johnson (J&J), where employees are encouraged to live by the corporate credo of honesty, integrity, and people-focus.[7]

Encouraging Stability. The presence of a strong corporate culture also encourages stability. The visible cultural artifacts provide clues for behavior. The values are passed on to new employees, and they are encouraged to abide by them. The assumptions provide the underlying guide for most of the organization's decision making over time. All these elements allow the organization to maintain some permanence.

Although the presence of newcomers at all levels always results in some change, a strong organizational culture eventually either socializes them or causes them to be rejected. An interesting example of the maintenance of stability is General Motors' (GM) purchase of EDS and Ross Perot's departure. GM's highly bureaucratic and sluggish culture survived by rejecting Perot, who did not fit well. This example also points to the negative aspects of stability brought about by a strong culture. These negative aspects will be discussed in a later section. Overall, part of the internal maintenance and smooth functioning of an organization depends on its culture, which provides members with an identity, encourages commitment, constitutes one of the bases for decision making and evaluation, and allows for some stability.

Defining and Adapting to the External Environment

To a great extent, the culture of an organization is created and evolves as a result of the organization's contact and interaction with its environment. The economic situation, the political climate, international relations, the industry's climate, the labor market, and competitors' products and marketing strategies, just to name a few, are all factors that influence the culture of an organization and limit and constrain its choices. Organizational culture and its underlying assumptions set the stage for the organization's reason for being in a given environment. An organization's identity allows it to position itself in society and in relation to its competitors and various constituents. Therefore, the culture of an organization is one of the factors that guides the firm's actions as it adapts and survives in its environment.

Defining the Environment. Once culture is formed, it plays a role in the way managers delineate and define the environment for their organization.[8] Either consciously or subconsciously, culture guides a manager's decision to enter a new market, to market a new product, to enter into a joint venture with a particular partner, or to merge with another firm. The resulting strategic decisions that are made, in turn, define the domain in which an organization operates. A highly ecologically conscious company may shy away from a joint venture with a company that has a reputation for environmental safety problems. For example, J&J has been reported not to market products that do not meet its strict quality standards.[9] J&J's corporate credo is one of the guides for such decisions.

Adapting to the Environment. In order to survive, an organization needs to adapt to its changing environment. The lack of fit to the environment either triggers attempts to change the culture or leads to organizational decline. Many organizations that have not adapted to their environment quickly have either disappeared or have been reorganized. An interesting example of the effect of lack of fit between environment and culture is the faith of the Professional Air Traffic Controllers Organization (PATCO), the air traffic controllers' union that was dismantled in 1981. The union's highly militant culture did not fit with the antiunion political climate. This lack of fit, among other things, led to the union's demise. Therefore, one of the functions of organizational culture is to help in the adaptation to the external environment. However, the degree to which the organization can change depends on the strength of its culture. The stronger the culture, the more likely it is to resist change. The factors that make a culture strong are the factors that are likely to cause resistance to change.

STRONG VERSUS WEAK CULTURES

Elements of a Strong Culture

Not all organizational cultures are equal. Some are strong and appear to have considerable power in influencing behavior; others are weak, almost imperceptible, and have little effect on employees and managers. Three elements compose the strength of a culture.[10] The first element is the number of shared beliefs, values, and assumptions, which will determine how thick a culture will be. The higher the number of shared assumptions, the thicker the culture. In thin cultures, few assumptions and values are commonly held.

The second element is the proportion of organizational members who share in the basic assumptions. The more people agree with various assumptions, the stronger they will be. And the third element is the clarity of the order of values and assumptions. If assumptions are clearly and specifically ordered, it is explicit which are central to the culture and the organization and which are minor. Central values are held and defended closely, whereas minor ones are more easily changed. In a strong culture, many values and assumptions are shared by a large proportion of organizational members. In addition, the shared assumptions are clearly ordered. Overall, the higher the number of clear assumptions shared by more people within an organization, the stronger the culture of that organization will be.

Several factors affect the strength of an organization's culture. Specifically, organizations with a homogeneous and stable membership that has long tenure are more likely to have a clearly ordered, large number of assumptions shared by most of their membership. In addition, the number of employees and geographic dispersion are also factors in the strength of culture. A smaller organization is likely to have a stronger culture, given that it is likely to be more homogeneous and therefore its members are more likely to share many assumptions and values. By the same token, if employees are not geographically dispersed, they are prone to develop a stronger sense of identity and a stronger culture. Another key factor is the extent of socialization efforts made to acculturate new employees. In some organizations, formal and informal behavioral norms, various cultural artifacts such as stories and symbols, as well as values and assumptions are clearly communicated to new employees, and they are encouraged and rewarded for adopting them. Other organizations expend less effort in trying to impart their culture to newcomers. The active socialization process is partly determined by the strength of the culture, but active socialization also becomes one of the factors that strengthens the corporate culture by communicating the culture to new employees.

IBM and Procter & Gamble (P&G) are often cited as two organizations with very strong corporate cultures. Assumptions about factors that are central to performance and success, the appropriate style of management, and employee conduct and career track, just to mention a few, are deep-rooted values shared by most members of the organization. Even outside observers can determine which values are central. For example, IBM has made a reputation by focusing on servicing its customers and providing them with quality products. It is equally clear that being at the cutting edge of innovation is not a strongly held value. Interestingly, although P&G and IBM provide examples of strong cultures, they are both large organizations that are geographically dispersed. However, they both make conscious efforts at maintaining stable membership and have very intricate socialization processes.

Benefits and Disadvantages of Strong Cultures

A strong culture provides members of an organization with a clear sense of identity. It clarifies behaviors and expectations and allows for ease of decision making. A strong culture can serve all the functions presented above and thereby afford the organization a clear competitive advantage. Given that many successful organizations have very strong cultures, it becomes highly tempting to associate success with a strong culture. A strong culture that supports and is congruent with strategy is one of the keys to success. For example, the customer-oriented culture of Wal-Mart has been touted as the key to its strategic success. On the other hand, incongruence of a strong culture with strategy can be deadly.

A strong culture can also be an impediment to success, as a strong culture resists change. If values are deeply shared by many people, they become difficult to change. Organizations with weak cultures may have an advantage in times of turbulence or decline when organizations are considering drastic strategic reorientation and massive internal changes. If values and assumptions are not deeply held, they will be more yielding and allow for the culture to change at the three levels described earlier.

A classic, often cited example of the disadvantages of a strong culture is the case of AT&T. Prior to the mid-1970s, AT&T's single, strong customer- and service-oriented culture supported the goals of a monopoly in a relatively stable environment. The strong culture not only supported AT&T's external corporate mission, but it also allowed it to maintain internal health. That same strong culture became a major handicap as the organization was required to undergo massive changes after the breakup. New environments called for new strategies, structures, managerial styles, and employee behaviors. The culture had to change to accommodate the transformations, and AT&T's strong culture became a major obstacle. Given that it had been so successful for such a long time, it was very difficult for organizational members to even recognize the need for change.

Another illustration of the disadvantages of a strong culture is GM. Its highly bureaucratic culture has not responded to either environmental or internal pressures for change. The short-lived success of the mid-1980s further reinforced and entrenched the existing culture and made managers discount or disregard all the outside factors that pointed to a need for modifying the culture. Other organizations whose strong cultures have been considered to have hindered change are Sears and Bank of America.[11]

Although a strong corporate culture supports the implementation of an organization's strategy and goals, it can also provide a major obstacle to new ideas and innovation and become a handicap in the organization's attempt to adapt to its external environment.

CHANGING ORGANIZATIONAL CULTURE

The culture of an organization undergoes gradual change as the organization adapts to various environmental and internal events. This gradual change is incremental and rarely involves considerable deviation from established patterns. Effecting massive organizational change is therefore very arduous. Changing the culture of an organization is as difficult as changing an individual's personality. Moreover, strong cultures will be more resistant to change than weak ones.

In order to change culture, all three of its levels have to change. Changing the first level of culture—which includes all artifacts, physical elements, dress codes, building decoration, symbols, logos, and even employee behaviors and speech patterns—is relatively easy. One key to such change is a new reward system. For example, cooperative behavior can be encouraged and taught if organizational reward systems encourage it. Employees come to learn that they will be rewarded for cooperation.

Changes in this first level, however, do not necessarily lead to changes in the second level, which includes values, or in the third level, which consists of basic assumptions. The latter two are much harder to modify. For example, although as a result of training and a new reward system employees may learn to behave more cooperatively, they may still value competition and consider it to be the key to success and high performance. In the short term, cooperation can become an espoused value. It can become a deeply held value only if it is proven successful over a period of time. In addition, values that are incongruent with basic assumptions are likely to lead to conflict and tension and are less likely to be adopted.

It is the sustained success of a new behavior (first level) that leads to the development of a new value (second level). If this new value is maintained and proven effective, it can lead to changes in some basic assumptions (third level). In the implementation of organizational change, a top-down approach is less likely to be effective, although it will lead to behavioral changes. Basic assumptions can only be changed if all organizational levels are committed to the change and adopt it as their own. The process will obviously take longer; however, employee participation leads to commitment to the development of new assumptions. Overall, although it may be relatively easy to change the observable and obvious elements of culture, it is very hard to modify the core of culture. Without the alteration of the basic cultural assumptions, the culture will only change superficially. Only with the long-term success of new behaviors will new assumptions develop. However, the deep-seated paradigms may prevent consideration of new behaviors and values, since they often lead to a biased interpretation of the success of new behaviors and therefore discourage their use.

Without major cultural change, considerable strategic change is likely to fail. Although the formulation of new strategy may be relatively easy, its successful implementation depends almost entirely on existing culture or, in many cases, on a change in the existing culture. But such a change is extremely difficult and can only be successful with extensive planning.

SUMMARY

The culture of an organization provides the bond and the identity that hold the members of that organization together. Although the superficial aspects of culture are easy to observe and even measure, a deep understanding of culture depends on access to the values that shape behavior and, more important, to the assumptions that provide the base for the values. The founders and leaders of an organization constitute one of the most powerful determinants of the basic assumptions that are at the heart of culture. Leaders influence the culture by being role models; by controlling the reward systems and hiring decisions; and by deciding on the structure, strategy, and physical setting of the organization.

Once a culture is in place, it helps the organization to function smoothly by providing a sense of identity and encouraging employee commitment. The culture also provides standards for decision making, which encourages stability in trying to define and adapt to the external environment. The strength of the culture of an organization will determine how well it fulfills its function. Strong cultures where many employees share many well-defined and well-ordered values are better able to support organizational performance. However, the strength of a culture can also impede vital change.

NOTES

1. For a thorough discussion of organizational culture, see T. E. Deal & A. A. Kennedy, *Corporate cultures: The rites and rituals of corporate life* (Reading, MA: Addison-Wesley, 1982).

2. E. H. Schein, *Organizational culture and leadership* (San Francisco: Jossey-Bass, 1985).

3. See Schein, *Organizational culture.*

4. See C. Argyris & D. A. Schon, *Organizational learning* (Reading, MA: Addison-Wesley, 1978).

5. E. Larson, Forever young, *Inc.*, July 1988, pp. 50–56.

6. See Corporate culture, *Business Week*, October 27, 1980, pp. 148–60; and K. Labich, Big changes at Big Brown, *Fortune*, January 18, 1988, p. 56.

7. See B. Dumaine, Corporate citizenship, *Fortune*, January 29, 1990, pp. 50, 54.

8. For a thorough discussion of the role of culture in the definition of the environment, see Schein, *Organizational culture.*

9. See Dumaine, Corporate citizenship.

10. See V. Sathe, *Culture and related corporate realities* (Homewood, IL: Irwin, 1985).

11. C. O'Reilly, Corporations, culture, and commitment: Motivation and social control in organizations, *California Management Review*, 31, (Summer 1989), pp. 9–25.

3

Corporate Strategies in Mergers

DIVERSIFICATION THROUGH MERGERS AND ACQUISITIONS

When CEOs are asked why they intend to acquire another firm, their responses are: (1) We intend to gain market share by eliminating a competitor in the same line of business; (2) we aim to expand into other relatively related fields where we can capitalize on one of our strengths, such as in marketing; (3) we intend to gain access to the valuable resources of one of our suppliers or customers; or (4) we need to diversify into other fields where opportunities for growth exist. These diversification strategies can be achieved through related, concentric, vertical, and unrelated mergers, respectively. Although some mergers are undertaken because of a whim, most CEOs with a corporate view of operations have very sound strategic reasons for acquiring another firm and can justify the merger in broad strategic strokes.

In this chapter, we will explore these types of mergers and the reasons for the success and failure of each. In addition to a corporate view of mergers, we will take a closer look at the merger process from the acquired firm's point of view. We will also examine many of the advantages and disadvantages of merger strategies.

Figure 3.1 depicts the four generic types of merger strategies explored in this book. Bargaining power, transfer of resources, personnel interaction, implementation time, profitability, and risk will be used to define each type of merger. *Bargaining power* refers to the amount of leverage the firms may have in negotiating with their suppliers and their buyers; the more bargaining power the firms have after the merger, the more competitive advantage they can gain over the competitors.[1] A major aim of

Figure 3.1
Degree of Relatedness and Difficulty of Implementation of Merger Strategies

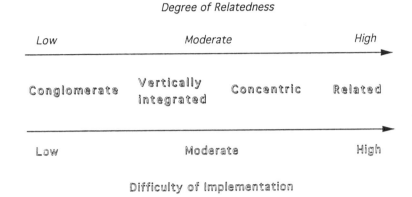

Degree of Relatedness

any merger is to transfer some resources, such as technology, among its divisions; therefore, the transfer of resources is an essential factor in the eventual success of any merger.

Every merger provides the managers and employees of both firms the opportunity to interact; the more this personnel interaction takes place, the higher the probability of conflict and cultural clashes. During a merger, executives strive to complete the deal as soon as possible so that the implementation phase can begin; therefore, there is relative implementation time urgency involved in mergers. Each merger type has a different level of profitability associated with it; some types are relatively more profitable than others. And finally, each type of merger strategy has a certain level of inherent risk that must be justified with higher returns. We will discuss these six factors in the context of each type of merger.

Overall, as the degree of relatedness increases, so does the degree of difficulty of implementing mergers. In conglomerate mergers, where very little personnel contact is needed, implementation of a merger is relatively easy to accomplish. At the other end of the spectrum, in related mergers, where the two firms are required to interact closely in order for the merger to succeed, implementation is relatively difficult to accomplish. Concentric and vertical mergers are in the medium range of personnel interaction and ease of implementation.

RELATED MERGERS

Related mergers are acquisitions made within the same industry. Here, companies buy either a direct competitor or one very closely related to their line of business. Conventional wisdom holds that the closer a firm stays to its line of business, the more knowledge its managers have about that business and, therefore, the higher the probability of success after the merger. This "stick-to-your-knitting" strategy has much merit.[2] Since the acquiring firm's managers already possess considerable knowledge about their industry and its idiosyncracies, they can identify the areas of savings and duplication prior to the merger. Consequently, they can consolidate the operations of the two firms after the merger and reap the savings. Table 3.1 presents a summary of the main advantages and disadvantages of the six key issues in related mergers.

Bargaining Power

A strategic advantage of related mergers is the bargaining power that the combined firm may gain in dealing with its suppliers and customers. Suppliers may provide the new firm with more favorable terms due to the increase in quantity of supplies ordered, or the credit suppliers may give more favorable credit terms to a firm with a larger asset base. In addition, the combined firm may be able to increase its products' prices or to reduce their quality, now that one less competitor exists in the market. In reality, however, many of these bargaining advantages are elusive and certainly not possible in the short term. After the merger, suppliers usually approach the new firm with caution and are very reluctant to give favorable credit terms. From their perspective, the new firm needs to prove that it can manage the crisis and the turmoil associated with the merger. The larger debt caused by most mergers also makes the suppliers wary of extending additional supplies on credit to the firm. The combined firm's customers may also balk at paying higher prices or accepting lower-quality products. Some of these bargaining advantages may be realized in the long run, only after the firm is able to prove that it is managing the implementation process successfully.

Transfer of Resources

Besides bargaining advantages, related mergers can benefit from the transfer of resources from one firm to the other. For example, the acquired firm may have some state-of-the-art technology that the acquirer firm can use, or the acquirer may transfer some special managerial skills to its acquired unit. Overall, the expectation of both parties in related mergers is that an extensive transfer of resources—besides monetary ones—takes place between the two organizations. Often, prior to the merger, the firms sign specific agreements on how extensively they will trade resources. If the transfer is total, then the acquired unit will become an integral part of the acquiring firm and lose its independence completely. Interestingly, many managers assume that since the acquired unit is in related businesses, it necessarily follows that it will lose its autonomy and be made an indis-

Table 3.1
Characteristics of Related Mergers

	ADVANTAGES	DISADVANTAGES
BARGAINING POWER	can lead to price concessions and better credit terms	short term, the merger crisis may make suppliers and buyers hesitant
TRANSFER OF RESOURCES	immediate transfer of physical assets such as technology	transfer of human resources may be difficult, leading to many quitting
PERSONNEL INTERACTION	required close interaction needed for synergy	required close interaction likely to lead to high conflict
IMPLEMENTATION TIME	none	up to seven years, which allows competitors to gain advantage
PROFITABILITY	on the average, more profitable than other types of mergers	may fail due to initial overpricing and later cultural clashes
RISK	may provide significant gains in market share; can allow for concentration of resources	risk is not diversified; "all eggs in the same basket"

tinguishable part of the parent firm. However, as we will explain in later chapters, total absorption of the acquired unit is just one of many options open to the acquirer.

Transfer of resources may be one of the most difficult tasks in any merger. Although physical assets can be transferred readily, the human resources may not accept the change willingly. Frequently, after a merger is announced, key managers and employees of one or both firms attempt to leave by entering the job market. Words such as "streamlining," "downsizing," "restructuring," and more recently, "right-sizing" indicate to these managers and employees that a period of turmoil is approaching, and many decide to bail out before it starts.

Personnel Interaction

Related mergers often lead to frequent and intense interaction between the personnel of the two firms.[3] Since the two firms are in related industries, and given the fact that many of their activities will be similar, there will be much interaction between the managers and employees of both firms. In fact, the day after the merger the human resources of both firms realize that now that they are combined, they need to work very closely with each other. The more contact these employees have with each other, the more conflict will result. On the other hand, a major advantage of combining the two organizations is that each will discover that the other partner has already solved many long-standing problems. For example, while the parent firm may still be struggling to find a solution to a packaging dilemma, the acquired firm may have found a perfect answer to the same question. Now that the two firms are combined, if managers and employees keep an open mind and do not engage in turf warfare, they will be able to attain synergy in their operations. After all, the goal of most related mergers is to achieve synergy from combining the operations of the two firms.

Related mergers are very hard to implement mainly due to the frequency and intensity of interaction between the employees of the two firms. There is much potential for cultural clashes and conflict as the two operations are being examined for areas of possible elimination.[4] Managers used to their own methods of operation will have to change quickly and adopt a new system. Then they have to take the new system and convince the rank and file that it is an improvement over the old system. Supervisors and line managers are the key personnel in the implementation of related mergers, since they control the daily interaction among the employees of the two firms being combined.

Implementation Time

Consolidating the different units of the two firms in a related merger takes many years to complete. In fact, researchers believe that it may take up to seven years for the combined firm to show any productivity gains. Meanwhile, competitors may be gaining advantage in the market. Unless the combined firm can quickly translate its larger size into a competitive advantage in, for example, economies of scale, the larger size of the combined firm is not an advantage per se.

In reality, due to its larger size, the firm becomes less responsive to its customers' needs. The recent merger of Manufacturers Hanover and Chemical banks is an example. Analysts believe that the recent merger of the two banks may be flawed for the same reasons: Their CEOs have cited the possible gain in economies of scale as a major reason for this merger as well as the "similarity" of their cultures. A closer look shows that the new giant bank will not be able to show any productivity gains for many years and that the cultures of the two banks are quite dissimilar.

Profitability

Not surprisingly, research shows that related diversification is, on the average, more profitable than other types.[5] However, this general rule does not explain why numerous related mergers fail to deliver on their preacquisition promises. Although the "stick-to-your-knitting" strategy prevents the CEOs from venturing into the unknown, it does not provide any guidelines on how a related merger must be managed for it to succeed. In addition, knowledge of industry does not automatically mean knowledge of culture. In fact, this type of merger may give a false sense of security to the managers of the acquiring firm. Since they already know much about the industry, they may decide not to engage in a full audit of the target firm and, as a result, may be surprised later how unhealthy their acquisition target is. It is worth mentioning that by *audit* we mean not only a financial audit—which is always conducted prior to a merger—but also a strategic, a cultural, a structural, and a leadership audit—which are not often conducted before a merger. In later chapters, we will explore these audits in detail.

Risk

The final factor to consider in mergers is the risk of merging with firms in the same industry. The entire future of the firm will be tied to the growth and competitive nature of one industry. In this respect, the combined firm loses flexibility in responding to environmental factors affecting its industry, whereas an unrelated merger may diversify such risk. Of course, assuming that the combined firm gains significant market share through the merger, how the firm manages the implementation of the merger and the fact that it can concentrate its resources in one industry may make it a significant player in that industry. This increase in market share may lead to higher profits in the long run.

In sum, although related mergers can have many benefits when managed properly, they are also one of the most difficult ones to implement. Their relatedness usually leads to attempts to combine the two firms. Combining their operations, however, requires careful analyses and planning, experience in merger implementation, and much patience and resources. It is the combining of the human resources that is often the most challenging. In other words, this strategy is not recommended for the "fainthearted"!

Overall, although related mergers are theoretically superior in performance to other types of mergers, they take the longest to show results and require skilled line managers and supervisors to implement the strategy.

CONCENTRIC MERGERS

When two firms from different but "adjacent" industries merge, a concentric merger has taken place. For example, if an auto manufacturer and a motorcycle manufacturer merge, the acquisition is a concentric one. Although both industries serve the transportation needs of their customers, the two are quite unique in their competitive structures. Usually, the merging firms determine some similarities in their technology or marketing[6] and attempt to capitalize on it by combining some but not all of their operations. The motorcycle firm may decide that the engine technology developed by the auto firm can improve its bikes and make them much more competitive in the market. Table 3.2 presents a summary of the main advantages and disadvantages of the six key issues in concentric mergers.

Bargaining Power

The merging firms can gain bargaining advantage over their suppliers in concentric mergers—but only under certain conditions. In technology-related mergers, for example, if sharing technology between the two firms leads to an increase in the quantity of supplies ordered related to that technology, then some bargaining advantage over the supplier can be gained. Also, if the technology- or market-related supplies can be readily obtained from many suppliers (i.e., the cost of switching to another supplier is low), then the merging firms can gain bargaining advantage. For example, if the additional trucks needed to distribute the combined goods of the two firms involved in a marketing-related merger can be obtained from any truck manufacturer, then the firm has bargaining advantage over the current supplier. It can negotiate lower prices and better services from that supplier.

Moreover, in concentric mergers, gaining bargaining advantage over the customers is possible if the products of the two firms can be "bundled" and sold as a set, and the customer cannot readily switch to another firm. For example, a computer hardware manufacturer can merge with a software manufacturer and subsequently require all its customers to use only that software. If its customers are very dependent on this specific brand of computers and cannot switch easily to another computer firm, then the merged firm will have bargaining power over these customers.

In most concentric mergers, however, gaining bargaining power over suppliers or customers is not easily obtained in the short term. As in related mergers, in concentric ones suppliers need to gain confidence in the long-

Table 3.2
Characteristics of Concentric Mergers

	ADVANTAGES	DISADVANTAGES
BARGAINING POWER	can lead to price concessions if use same supplies and bundle products	short term, the merger crisis will make suppliers and buyers hesitant; bundling can lead to antitrust violations
TRANSFER OF RESOURCES	prior agreement states timetable for transfer of resources	transfer of human resources may be difficult due to lack of industry expertise
PERSONNEL INTERACTION	moderate interaction; joint teams to solve problems	some cultural clashes; turf warfare is possible
IMPLEMENTATION TIME	relatively quick--within 1-2 years	none
PROFITABILITY	more than vertical and conglomerate	less than related; in the long run, meddling may cause losses and less profit
RISK	more diversified and less dependent on one industry	more risk due to need for management attention to each industry fluctuation

term viability of the merged firms before they are willing to extend any credit. In fact, the sense of crisis that follows mergers causes bargaining disadvantage for the merged firms. In addition, if the combined firm becomes a significant player in the industry, its bundling practices may violate antitrust regulations.

Transfer of Resources

In concentric mergers, the selective transfer of resources from one firm to the other is usually the primary purpose of the merger. Most firms know in advance what skills and resources they intend to share or transfer to the other firm. Usually, the terms of the merger contracts specify a timetable for these transfers. Most companies are adept at relocating technology or marketing-related assets. Many firms have experts who can plan and administer these transfers painlessly.

However, despite the merger agreements and just like in related mergers, in concentric mergers transferring human resources from one unit to the other often results in very high levels of resistance by employees and managers. For example, if the acquiring firm sends a team of managers to the acquired unit, these managers will often face resistance from the personnel of the acquired firm, unless the acquired firm's human resources agree in advance to such transfer. Moreover, since many merger agreements are negotiated in secret, most employees are surprised by the transfer agreements related to personnel and thus resist them.

Personnel Interaction

The frequency and intensity of personnel interaction in concentric mergers are usually less than in related mergers. Although many sources of synergy will be explored by the partners, overall there is an expectation on both sides that each will not meddle in the other's affairs. Key managers and employees will become members of joint committees and meet frequently to find solutions to merger problems. At the same time, each side is expected to keep its autonomy and run its business the way it sees fit. Going back to the merger example above, teams of managers from the motorcycle unit and the auto unit may meet to resolve some technology or marketing-related problem; but each of the units is expected to manage its business according to the norms of its own industry. This arm's length relationship will reduce the tendency for each partner to meddle in the affairs of the other and will reduce cultural clashes.[7] It will also reduce the possibility of the acquired unit's key employees leaving as a result of such meddling.

Since the two firms may have different cultures, managers need to know how to manage the differences between the cultures. For example, the degree of emphasis each organization puts on employee training and indoctrination, job rotation and enrichment, or rites and rituals may vary. Cultural differences manifest themselves in the day-to-day operations of each organization, and the acquirers need to first become aware of these differences and then devise a strategy to manage them. In later chapters, we will explore some of these strategies.

Implementation Time

Since in concentric mergers only selective assets or operations will be combined, the time frame for implementation is much shorter than in related mergers. Usually within a year or two of the merger, the operations have been consolidated and the firm can see some tangible results. For example, if two firms decide to consolidate their marketing functions only, this can be accomplished quickly if both firms perceive some gains resulting from the merger. Of course, the timetable expands if conflict arises from disagreements. But if each party perceives the merger as being equally, mutually beneficial, then many obstacles to implementation can be removed quickly.

Profitability

Although concentric diversifications have been less profitable than related ones, on the average, they are more profitable than vertical and unrelated diversifications—the reason being that the acquiring firms know exactly what they want from their target firms and often leave the rest of the organization intact. Using the marketing consolidation example again, once the two firms merge and combine their marketing functions, the other activities of the two firms remain separate. However, the tendency to meddle in the affairs of the acquired firms is still very high for the acquirers. Although they may leave the acquired units autonomous initially, in the long run they impose a host of financial, strategic, and human resources systems on the purchased units and in effect take away their autonomy. This meddling will inevitably cause resentment among the managers and the employees of the acquired firms and leads to loss of productivity and perhaps less profits for all.

Risk

Concentric mergers diversify the overall portfolio of the organization, and the firm becomes less dependent on one industry. Consequently, however, the organization needs to worry about the fortunes of two industries. Unlike a portfolio of stocks that a firm does not need to worry about and can trade quickly, a portfolio of two concentric businesses requires management attention. Using the example of the merging auto and motorcycle manufacturers discussed earlier, now the combined firm needs to monitor the competitiveness of two businesses, keep tabs on a number of worldwide rivals and their strategic plans and innovations, and decide to which business it should allocate more resources.

Overall, concentric mergers are easier to implement than related mergers. The fact that most of the operations of the acquired unit will be kept separate will minimize personnel interaction and cultural clashes and conflict. At the same time, they seem to be less profitable than related mergers.

An essential factor in the success of concentric mergers is the premerger agreement detailing which operations will be solidified and which will remain autonomous.

VERTICAL MERGERS

Many firms attempt to buy one of their suppliers (backward merger) or merge with one of their customer firms (forward merger). These types of mergers are called vertical mergers. The motivation for buying a supplier can be to guarantee availability of some scarce resource on which the firm is highly dependent.[8] For example, DuPont purchased Conoco mainly to guarantee itself a steady stream of crude oil on which its petrochemical plants are dependent. Another motivation for a backward merger can be to obtain cheaper supplies, since no profit margin is added to the products of an internal supplier. On the other hand, the firm may choose to merge forward in order to absorb the margin in its customer's line of business. For example, a lobster-fishing firm may decide that the value added to its product at the retail level is substantial and thus buy the restaurant to which it sells its product. Table 3.3 presents a summary of the main advantages and disadvantages of the six key issues in vertical mergers.

Bargaining Power

Vertical mergers can increase the bargaining power of the combined firm. If by merging vertically a firm brings more stability to its core business, then it can demand better terms from its suppliers. In the lobster firm, for instance, if buying a restaurant guarantees a ready market for the firm, then suppliers can be asked to provide more lenient credit terms. Unlike the two other types of mergers discussed, in vertical mergers the gain in bargaining power can be achieved relatively quickly. On the other hand, if the industry is relatively turbulent, the bargaining power of the combined firm may not be affected.

Transfer of Resources

Vertical mergers do not normally involve any transfer of resources, except perhaps monetary ones. The acquired firm becomes part of the ac-

Table 3.3
Characteristics of Vertical Mergers

	ADVANTAGES	DISADVANTAGES
BARGAINING POWER	can lead to price concessions quickly	if industry is turbulent, can lead to no increase in bargaining power
TRANSFER OF RESOURCES	only financial resources are transferred	can refocus the business without management expertise
PERSONNEL INTERACTION	minimal interaction is required	forcing of close interaction can lead to high conflict
IMPLEMENTATION TIME	relatively quick	none
PROFITABILITY	can absorb the acquired unit's margin	on the average, less profitable than other types of mergers
RISK	good risk in stable market	"all eggs in the same basket"; risky in early and late stages of the product life cycle

quirer's corporate umbrella and deals partly or exclusively with the parent firm.

However, in some situations more resources are transferred from the parent firm to the acquired unit. For example, if for some strategic reason the acquirer decides that the business of the other unit is so lucrative that it should refocus its own corporate efforts and make the purchased business its main line of business, then it has changed its center of gravity. This change in the center of gravity occurred when General Mills, through mergers, moved from being a flour miller to a producer of consumer food products.[9] With the change in the center of gravity, more resources can be allocated to the new area of emphasis and even managers may be transferred from the acquirer to the acquired firm. Interestingly, in some vertical mergers the change in center of gravity may happen so gradually that managers may not even be aware of this refocusing of corporate mission and later discover themselves in another business.

Personnel Interaction

In vertical mergers, since the two businesses are in separate industries, each with its own norms and values, the opportunity for personnel interaction is minimal. Most of the interaction takes place at the corporate level, where price, quality, and other characteristics of the acquired firm's products are negotiated. Thus, it is not important how similar or dissimilar the cultures of the two firms are. The way each business conducts its day-to-day affairs—from its dress codes and norms of conduct to its benefits and rewards systems—may differ greatly or may be quite similar.

Since the purpose of the merger is to have an arm's length relationship with the acquired firm and, for example, mainly transfer its finished goods to the acquiring firm, then the differences in the two cultures should not cause conflict between the firms' personnel. Personnel from the two firms only interact when absolutely necessary. On the other hand, if closer strategic and functional ties are envisioned in the long run, then cultural differences need to be closely monitored and managed. In later chapters, we will discuss how differences may be managed.

Implementation Time

Compared with related and concentric mergers, vertical mergers can be implemented very quickly. In the short run, no major changes in the two firms' relationship may be necessary, and the goods from one unit are simply delivered to the other firm. In the long run, however, as new systems such as accounting, strategic planning, and human resources planning are passed on to the acquired unit, the relationship may evolve and much closer ties between the two units may result.

Profitability

In theory, vertical mergers allow a firm to absorb its acquisition's margin and thus become more profitable. In practice, however, research shows that on the average vertically diversified firms have been much less profitable than those involved in related and concentric diversifications. It seems that by acquiring a supplier, for example, the combined firm is suddenly thrown into another industry that has different competitors and different ways of conducting business. Suddenly, corporate managers may be faced with a much higher degree of competitive complexity than they may be accustomed to.

In addition, by acquiring a supplier, there is always the danger of over-buying supplies, depending on the production capacity of the acquired firm. Moreover, if the competitive nature of the industry changes, the acquired firm will be stuck with a supplier that it may not need any longer. Also, innovation in the acquired firm may suffer since the selling is done internally, and the firm may become isolated from the competitive environment.

Risk

Vertical mergers tie the fortunes of the combined firm to one line of products. If the market is stable and growing, and the merger is implemented properly, it can be quite successful. However, if the market is in its early stages of the life cycle or in the decline stage, vertical mergers lead to loss of flexibility and can be risky ventures. This type of merger does not have the benefits of diversifying risk discussed in concentric mergers. Rather, in vertical mergers, the risk of dependence on one industry is not really diversified by merging with a supplier or a customer firm since the combined firm is still dependent on one line of products.

In general, vertical mergers can be quite successful if the market is stable and growing. The objective of managers in vertical mergers should be to allow only minimal contact between the personnel of the two firms, thus minimizing conflict and cultural clashes. If the competitive nature of the industry changes and the market becomes more turbulent, vertical acquisitions should be evaluated for possible sale.

CONGLOMERATE MERGERS

One of the most popular types of mergers in the 1950s and the 1960s was conglomerate mergers. Based on the concept of diversifying industry- and product-related risks, conglomerate mergers involve the purchase of as many unrelated businesses as possible. Beatrice Foods and ITT are good examples of firms following this strategy. Although not as popular these days, conglomerate mergers are still a very viable option for firms intending to diversify.

Since many businesses are cyclical, one can theoretically build a portfolio of countercyclical businesses and thus have a steady stream of cash flow. In practice, however, finding countercyclical businesses is no easy task. Harder still is making sure that each business in the portfolio is competitive and profitable. Table 3.4 presents a summary of the main advantages and disadvantages of the six key issues in conglomerate mergers.

Table 3.4
Characteristics of Conglomerate Mergers

	ADVANTAGES	DISADVANTAGES
BARGAINING POWER	marginal gains in the short term	excessive size can reduce bargaining power
TRANSFER OF RESOURCES	short-term transfers only; primarily financial resources	long-term managerial and other control systems may be transferred
PERSONNEL INTERACTION	minimal interaction required	forcing close interaction may lead to high conflict
IMPLEMENTATION TIME	very quick	none
PROFITABILITY	higher than vertical mergers	lower than related and concentric mergers
RISK	depends on industry	overall business risk increases

Bargaining Power

Most firms that follow a conglomerate merger strategy are already a conglomeration of unrelated businesses. As a result of their size, therefore, when a new acquisition is made, some marginal gains in bargaining power are achieved for the combined firm. The gain becomes more significant if the acquired firm's size is large relative to the size of the conglomerate. Suppliers are more willing to extend credit to a large conglomerate, knowing that to a certain extent the firm is isolated from downturns in business conditions. However, if the acquisition is perceived as adding size at the expense of competitive advantage, then the combined firm's bargaining power is reduced.

Transfer of Resources

Since the businesses involved in a conglomerate merger are by definition unrelated, the major resource transferred across the units is monetary. Frequently, an acquired unit receives an infusion of cash from the parent firm. The expectation of a parent firm in this type of merger is for its acquired unit to achieve profitability as soon as possible. The expectation of the acquired unit is for the parent firm to give it autonomy and support it financially.

In reality, however, parent firms frequently force other transfers of resources. They inundate the acquired unit with financial reporting and personnel-related paperwork. Some also attempt to forge a new mission for the acquired unit with the hope that it will be more in line with the overall strategic direction of the conglomerate. And as a final blow to the autonomy of the acquired unit, once in a while the parent firm may send a new top management team from headquarters to the unit to manage it. This frequently happens if the acquired unit has been lagging in profitability compared with the other businesses within the conglomerate. Consequently, much more than just financial resources are transferred to the acquired unit.

Personnel Interaction

By definition, the conglomerate firm is composed of businesses from very different industries. The day-to-day norms of each business will vary as well as each's reward and compensation system. Opportunities for personnel interaction between firms is very limited, as is the possibility of conflict and cultural clashes. As long as the businesses are managed as separate entities, and financial resources are the only link between the acquired unit and the corporate office, implementation of the merger should proceed smoothly. Most conglomerates abide by this rule in the short run. In the long run, however, some attempt to impose uniform standards from the headquarters. These standards will cause major conflicts with the acquired unit's personnel.

Implementation Time

Conglomerate mergers are probably the quickest mergers to implement. Since no transfer of real assets takes place, implementation evolves around consolidation of financial reporting and personnel systems. Typically, the managers of the acquired unit act as if nothing has changed and operate their unit accordingly. The corporate office acts as an internal bank, securing financial resources for the unit at favorable rates. In the long run, however, the corporate office may change its strategy and seek closer ties among all the businesses in its portfolio. In such a case, the mergers will become more concentric, and many of the issues discussed in the section on concentric mergers will apply to the situation.

Profitability

Conglomerates have lagged in profitability when compared with related and concentric diversifiers. Partly due to the countercyclical characteristics of their portfolio, some units are always in an industrywide recession and thus negatively affect the overall performance of the conglomerate. In addition, many experts believe that building such a large portfolio of unrelated businesses is unwise since its size makes it unmanageable. If the only advantage of a conglomerate is to acquire funds at a cheaper rate, then no synergies among its businesses exist. Therefore, when the profitability of a group of these conglomerates is compared with the return of a group of closely related firms, where synergies in many aspects of the operations can be achieved, the conglomerates show less profitability.[10] It should be noted, however, that there are some very profitable conglomerates that acquire already successful businesses, support them with funds, and leave them autonomous to continue their profitability.

Risk

Conglomerate mergers attempt to reduce the industry- and product-related risks of a firm, yet they inevitably increase the size and reduce the strategic flexibility of the firm. In fact, some conglomerates are so large and unwieldy that market analysts give them a higher risk factor (i.e., beta) than a related diversifier. If the acquired unit is perceived as a competitively strong company within its own industry, and the acquirer is willing to allow it to remain autonomous and provide it with financial resources, then the market will perceive the merger as positive for the combined firm.

Overall, conglomerate mergers can be very profitable if the contact among the personnel of the firm is minimized and only financial resources are shared. When conglomerates lose sight of this initial strategy and attempt to forge closer ties among their businesses, major conflict will result, which can affect the success of conglomerate mergers.

SUMMARY

In this chapter we explained each type of merger strategy and the advantages and disadvantages associated with their six key issues. While related mergers are on the average more profitable, they are the hardest to implement. Conglomerate mergers are the easiest to implement, yet they are usually less profitable. Corporate mission statements usually dictate which type of merger strategy will be pursued by the firm. The choice of the merger strategy will have implications for the structure of the firm, its culture, and its leadership. These issues will be explored in the next few chapters.

NOTES

1. M. E. Porter, *Competitive strategy* (New York: Free Press, 1980).

2. R. P. Rumelt, *Strategy, structure, and economic performance* (Boston, MA: Harvard Business School Press, 1974).

3. A. Nahavandi & A. R. Malekzadeh, Acculturation in mergers and acquisitions, *Academy of Management Review*, 13, no. 1 (1988), pp. 79–90.

4. For some excellent examples of these conflicts in mergers, see A. F. Buono & J. L. Bowditch, *The human side of mergers and acquisitions* (San Francisco: Jossey-Bass, 1989).

5. See Rumelt, *Strategy*.

6. H. I. Ansoff, *Corporate strategy: An analytic approach to business policy for growth and expansion* (New York: McGraw-Hill, 1965).

7. See A. R. Malekzadeh & A. Nahavandi, Making mergers work by managing the cultures, *Journal of Business Strategy*, May/June 1990, pp. 55–57.

8. Many authors have written on the overall strategy of vertical integration. For example, see K. R. Harrigan, *Strategies for vertical integration* (Lexington, MA: Lexington Books, 1983).

9. J. R. Galbraith, Strategy and organization planning, *Human Resource Management*, 22, nos. 1/2 (1983), pp. 64–77.

10. See Rumelt, *Strategy*.

4

Merging of Structures

The structure of a firm refers to the way in which its human resources are organized and entails the hierarchy, departmentation, span of control, and integration among the various units. The structure and design of an organization are the result of its external environment, its size, its technology, its goals, and its leadership. Additionally, culture and strategy play a crucial role. Of particular interest in mergers is the link between structure and strategy, as the fit between them is essential to organizational performance. Undertaking a merger involves combining two organizations, which necessarily affects the structure of the two merger partners. As organizations merge, reporting relationships change, spans of control are modified, and departmental functions are altered. In most mergers, these changes come in the face of relatively little premerger planning. Although many firms consider the implications of structural change on their organization, often such analysis is cursory and superficial.

This chapter will introduce the major elements of structure, then explore the relationship among structure, strategy, and culture. Finally, the structural changes within each type of merger strategy presented in the previous chapter will be discussed.

DIMENSIONS OF STRUCTURE

Structure has numerous dimensions: formalization, specialization, standardization, hierarchy of authority, complexity, centralization, professionalism, and personnel ratios. Among them, complexity, formalization, and centralization are focal to our discussion of mergers (see Figure 4.1).

Figure 4.1
Dimensions of Structure

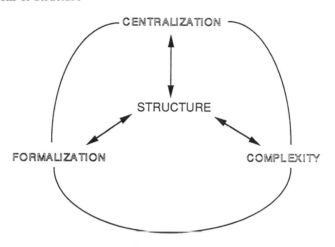

Complexity

Complexity refers to the number and variety of hierarchical layers, job titles, and divisions and departments within an organization.[1] The more layers and divisions, the higher the complexity of an organization. It is interesting to note that the level of complexity may vary within the same firm. For example, the legal department may have many layers of lawyers and staff members servicing the legal needs of different regions of the country, whereas manufacturing may have only one location with two hierarchical levels.

Formalization

Formalization refers to the number and content of rules and regulations present within an organization.[2] The more written rules, standard operating procedures, and policy manuals, the more formal an organization. The degree of formalization determines how many decisions are preprogrammed, since rules and manuals can replace managerial decision making. Highly formalized structures lead to routine work and activity. In formal organizations, behaviors and activities are predetermined since they are described in some document. Employee freedom in decision making and behavior is therefore highly limited. Additionally, formalization often leads to impersonality for both employees and customers.

Centralization

Centralization refers to the distribution of power and decision making within an organization.[3] The less the number of groups and levels involved in decision making, the more centralized a firm. In centralized organizations, a large majority of all decisions are made by top managers. In decentralized organizations, on the other hand, decisions are delegated or pushed down to lower levels.

DETERMINANTS OF STRUCTURE

There has been considerable research regarding the factors that determine, and are determined by, the structure and design of an organization. The factors considered most often are size, technology, strategy, external environment, and most recently, culture and leadership. Evidence can be found supporting the position that these elements determine structure and that structure determines them. So there is a circular relationship among them. They all mutually influence and limit one another. The structure of an organization depends on its environment, technology, strategy, and so on. On the other hand, once a structure is in place, it confines the options available in terms of technology, strategy, and many of the other elements. We will focus on the elements of size, culture, leadership, and strategy, as they are most central to mergers (see Figure 4.2).

Size

The larger an organization, the more likely it is to be complex and formal. For example, large universities are known for the presence of a sizable number of rules and manuals governing all aspects of student activities. Universities are also highly complex, with a variety of departments and divisions all attempting to serve the students. Many potential students shy away from the complexity and impersonality of large universities and opt for smaller ones. Smaller organizations can function without the many layers of managers and multiple procedures and, therefore, can often be more personal and responsive.

Contrary to the relationship of size and formalization and complexity, larger size usually forces decentralization. For example, a large, geographically dispersed conglomerate will have to decentralize decision making to some extent. Decisions regarding day-to-day activities have to be made within each local unit. Formalized procedures also reduce the need for direct control. At the other end of the continuum, in a small, single-business organization, top managers are likely to maintain active control of most of the decisions.

The structure of an organization can also become a factor in allowing

Figure 4.2
Determinants of Structure

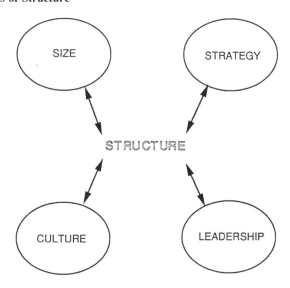

an organization to grow. For example, an organization with a functional structure may have trouble managing multiple products and constituents. In order to allow for diversification of its products, which are likely to lead to an increase in size, the structure has to be changed. Additionally, if new products require considerable interaction and cooperation among departments, the functional structure is likely to be inappropriate. If the structure is not changed, growth is likely to be stifled. Therefore, the structure affects the size in the same way that size originally determined the structure.

Culture

Culture and structure are inseparable, since structure is one of the major manifestations of culture. As discussed in Chapter 2, the culture of an organization is one of the factors that determines the relationship among employees and managers. As with the other elements, however, the culture of an organization may also be the result of structure. For example, in a highly centralized organization, the implementation of participative management and employee empowerment will be impossible without a change in the structure. Thus, the two elements are totally intertwined.

Leadership

The effect of leadership on organizations, particularly as it relates to mergers, will be discussed at length in Chapter 6. Although not studied as extensively, it has been found that leader personal characteristics affect the structure of an organization. For example, a highly authoritarian, control-oriented executive is likely to centralize his or her organization. The development of many rules and regulations and manuals will also reinforce control, and so they are likely to be present. On the other hand, a participative leader will delegate many of the decisions and may even be less likely to demand the development of uniform handbooks.

Consequently, the style and personality of the leader are likely to be at least partly reflected in the structure of the organization. It is important to note the reverse relationship: The structure of a firm may be one of the factors that influences the choice of leader. An organization that is very informal and decentralized is likely to consciously or unconsciously recruit and select CEOs who have similar philosophies. Dial Corporation (formerly Greyhound Corporation), which used to be part of ITT, selected John Tees as its CEO. Tees's style is known to mirror that of ITT's founder. The same firm is highly unlikely to select a hands-off manager unless a major crisis occurs, requiring a major shakeup.

Strategy

There has been much debate about the direction of the relationship between structure and strategy. In the 1920s, the common assumption was that structure followed the development of strategy. Strategy was devised and led to the formation of a structure that matched. An often-used example is the case of General Motors, which at the time devised the divisional structure to support its new strategy of competing product lines. In the case of GM, structure followed strategy. However, in the 1960s the position changed. Many companies found that their structure interfered with the implementation of their strategies. As a result, strategy was said to have to follow structure rather than the other way around. Consider, for example, the problems IBM faced in trying to develop its version of personal computers (PCs). IBM found that its structure was not supporting its new strategy. Apple's structure, on the other hand, lent itself well to the innovation and risk taking necessary to develop the newly developed PCs.

Much of the debate regarding the link between strategy and structure has been laid to rest with the current position that the relationship between them is circular. They mutually affect each other. They need to complement (match) one another for the organization to perform well. In new, young organizations, strategy can determine structure; the 1920s position therefore applies. Once a structure is in place, however, it limits the strategic alternatives available to the organization. A highly formalized, complex organization may, for example, have trouble being flexible and innovative. In order to overcome the limits of its bureaucratic structure, IBM had to circumvent its hierarchy and develop its PC outside. Therefore, a drastic change in strategy in an established organization requires an equally radical change in structure, as the match between the two elements is essential to performance.

The three dimensions of structure and their related organizational elements undergo considerable change in a merger. Each type of merger, however, produces different types and amounts of reorganization of human resources. The type of merger is one of the primary determinants of the type of structural change. However, leadership and managerial styles also play a central role.

STRUCTURAL CHANGES IN RELATED MERGERS

As described in Chapter 3, a related merger involves considerable interaction between the employees of the two firms. The interaction is based on the need to achieve synergy by reducing duplication. As a result, a related merger is likely to evoke considerable structural change for both merger partners.

Complexity

As soon as a merger is completed, the acquired unit has to be combined with the existing structure of the acquiring firm. As a result, the level of complexity within both organizations changes. Most of the departments need to be combined quickly, whereas a few may remain separate. A number of job titles will be altered, the reporting relationships of managers will change, and layers of hierarchy may be added. Although it may sound theoretically simple to combine a new acquisition with the existing organization, in reality, this is perhaps the hardest and the most time-consuming phase of implementing a merger.[4]

The division of labor in the two firms is likely to be very different. For example, if functioning as the reservation department of an airline employees were very specialized in their tasks, now as part of the parent firm's airline reservation department they may have to change their work routines and tasks completely and become generalists. The issue here is not whether being a generalist is better than being a specialist. Rather, the point is that the transformation in the nature of the work will immediately and profoundly affect the productivity of the managers and the employees of the acquired firm and, by association, and productivity of other managers and employees.

Formalization

Formalization within the organization may not change immediately after the merger, but it is likely to do so in the long run. Once the merger is consummated, the parent firm may not, for example, immediately attempt to formalize the decision-making procedures of the acquired unit. However, in spite of promises of noninterference, the acquiring firm may start to issue rules regulating the behavior of the managers and employees of the new unit. Whether formalization will increase or decrease depends on the structure of the acquirer. Regardless, the acquired unit is likely to receive a large set of new directives. These rules are often issued without regard for the adverse effect they may have on the unit's employees.

Overall, there is much pressure to change the behavior of the acquired unit in related mergers. The idea here is not to force the new unit to add to its rules and regulations. Rather, the parent firm prefers the acquired unit to have the *same* rules and procedures as it does. The change in procedures will often be perceived by members of the acquired unit as an increase in rules and regulations. After the merger, the seemingly mundane rules of conduct suddenly become a major source of employee complaints. The parent firm views the situation as one of equity: All employees should adhere to the same rules. Yet the acquired unit's managers and employees view the situation as unnecessary change imposed by the parent firm. It is, therefore, very important to prepare the new unit's employees for the upcoming changes in their day-to-day routine.

The synergy that is the goal of related mergers partly relies on a reduction in operating costs. The savings expected from combining the firms will only be realized if the duplicate operations of the two firms are combined, and since these firms are in related businesses, obviously there will be many redundant departments. Once managers start to combine the operations of the two units, there is a tendency to impose the parent firm's rules on the acquired firm rather than choosing the best set of rules.

At the beginning of the chapter we mentioned that the more regard the firm has for its human resources, the less the number of preprogrammed decisions. Yet even in mergers where human resources are the most valuable assets being transferred, the imposition of rules that negate the level of expertise of the employees takes place. For example, in a related merger between two accounting firms, the fact that the acquired unit had highly trained professionals may be mentioned as the primary reason for the merger. Nonetheless, as soon as the merger is consummated, the same highly trained professionals are subjected to numerous headquarter-imposed rules. The result can be frustrated and angry accountants who decry their lack of autonomy and their loss of freedom in making judgments in a judgment-based profession.

Centralization

Given that related mergers require consolidation of many departments and units of the two organizations, the acquired unit is likely to experience an increase in the degree of centralization. As was the case with formalization, the change in the reporting relationship and having to report to the new parent firm may be perceived as an increase in centralization and a loss of independence. However, in reality, the new firm may not be much more centralized. The accounting example presented above is one instance of operating decisions being imposed by the parent firm. In other cases, executives in the parent firm may make strategic decisions without input from the acquired unit's key people, yet the decisions may profoundly affect the acquired unit and its operations.

The culture of the acquiring organization is one of the key factors in determining how much autonomy the acquired unit is given. We have seen that after a related merger if the existing culture of the firms allowed for decentralization of decision making, the combined operation was given a relatively high amount of autonomy. On the other hand, if the existing culture was highly centralized, the same norms and practices were continued despite what the acquired unit desired. In effect, in both cases the parent firm's decision-making norms are imposed on the acquired unit regardless of what is best for the overall organization, thereby not only centralizing decision making but also increasing formalization.

STRUCTURAL CHANGES IN CONCENTRIC MERGERS

Complexity

Concentric mergers tend to increase the level of structural complexity for both merger partners. Here, managers need to decide which departments and units have to be completely absorbed, which remain closely connected but not absorbed, and which, if any, will function relatively independently. The absorbed units' managers and employees will go through the same structural transformation that was mentioned for employees in related mergers; the changes will be perceived as in increase in complexity. For the employees of closely connected departments, the level of complexity is likely to increase as several layers of hierarchy will become overlapping. On the other hand, for the newly purchased units that are kept under the corporate umbrella but not fully absorbed, the level of complexity may not change considerably. The reporting relationships are likely to remain the same for all but the top layers of the unit.

Formalization

The formalization of rules and regulations in concentric mergers follows many of the same patterns as those discussed for related mergers. Those units that have to be fully combined will have to adopt all the regulations of the acquiring firm's unit and, in addition, adhere to the corporate rules and standards. The net effect is that the acquired unit will change most if not all of its operating norms and practices. However, those units that do not have a counterpart within the parent firm are likely to keep most of their operating autonomy by adhering only to corporate standards. For example, a firm that always farmed out its research and development (R&D) not acquires an R&D firm. The new unit will be asked to adhere to corporate standards and norms but will have relative autonomy at the operating level. In this situation, the parent firm is often willing, at least for the short term, not to formalize the day-to-day operations of the new unit, especially if the unit shows positive financial results. In the long run, however, the slow stream of standards and regulations will have a cumulative effect on ensuring the conformity of the acquired unit with corporate standards.

Centralization

The degree of centralization in concentric mergers is likely to be different for each department of the acquired firm, depending on the extent of consolidation that is imposed. Mainly due to the fact that the operations of the two firms differ, the parent firm usually allows for relative decentralization in units for which there is no counterpart; yet the parent firm formulates the strategic direction of the corporation, thereby increasing centralization, at least to some extent, for all the various parts of the acquired unit.

STRUCTURAL CHANGES IN VERTICAL MERGERS

Complexity

When firms merge with a buyer or a supplier firm, redesigning the corporate structure is relatively easy. The new unit is usually added as a division to the organization chart and left relatively independent in decision making. If, for example, the firm were a supplier, now it may become the internal supplier for the resources the parent firm needs. Thus, in the short run, the merger usually does not change the degree of complexity to a very large extent. In the long run, however, many of the changes mentioned as occurring in concentric mergers may take place in vertical mergers as well.

With the addition of a new division, the level of complexity at the corporate level increases moderately. New reporting relationships have to be designed, and the corporate office may have to be reorganized to accommodate the new acquisition. If the new unit is a supplier, corporate executives will decide whether the unit's products should be sold externally to other firms in the market or sold internally or whether a combination of the two strategies is appropriate. The strategic implications of providing competitors with the firm's product must be weighed against the extra cost of keeping production below optimum level in order to produce for internal use only.

If the new unit is the buyer of the firm's products, once again the corporate office will decide whether or not the acquired unit should be the exclusive buyer for the parent firm's products. In addition, the acquired unit needs to know whether it can buy its supplies from the open market or whether it has to buy exclusively from the parent firm. Once these strategic decisions are made, the parent firm tends to give relative autonomy to the acquired unit.

Formalization

In vertical mergers, the level of formalization of rules and regulations is prone to increase to a lesser extent than in the other types of mergers described earlier. The new unit will, of course, have to adopt the corporate rules and reporting systems; but at the unit level, it will have operating autonomy to conduct its business. Most corporate executives realize that since the acquired firm is from a different industry, the less formalized the structure is, the more the acquired firm's managers' freedom to deal with their own industry's norms. This flexibility will allow the unit to design an optimum strategy to compete with its strongest competitors. However, acquiring firms often disregard the competitive environment of the acquired unit and overregulate what it can and cannot do. Obviously, such a tactic will lead to loss of competitive advantage for the unit.

Centralization

Given the often very different industries of the two merger partners in a vertical integration (VI) merger, the acquiring firm should ideally allow its acquisition a high degree of independence in decision making. Centralization of decision making and power may lead to lack of competitiveness for the acquired unit. In Chapter 3, we mentioned that the more the firm centralizes decision making, the less regard it has for the expertise of its personnel. Overcentralization can be detrimental to vertical mergers.

Given the lack of expertise of the corporate executives concerning the acquired unit's industry, most of the strategic decisions should be made by the unit's managers. For example, if a soft drink company decides to purchase one of its major suppliers, such as a sugar firm, its corporate executives will not have the knowledge to manage the sugar unit centrally. The expertise to manage the unit strategically lies with the managers of the sugar unit. Additionally, being part of a corporate umbrella may stifle innovation within the acquired unit. If too much centralization takes places, and many of the routine decisions that used to be made at the unit level now require corporate approval, the willingness to take risk and innovate may suffer at the unit. As a result, the acquired unit may soon lose its competitive advantage to other firms that may be more entrepreneurial and make strategic decisions faster.

STRUCTURAL CHANGES IN CONGLOMERATE MERGERS

By definition, conglomerate mergers should engender relatively little structural change for both merger partners. The acquired unit becomes part of the parent firm's corporate financial umbrella without undergoing a high degree of internal changes.

Complexity

In conglomerate mergers, the change in complexity most likely occurs only at the top levels for both merger partners. Based on our discussion of this issue in Chapter 3, the acquired unit should be autonomous to pursue its strategic mission without any interference from headquarters. However, with the addition of the new unit, the coordination-and-control tasks of the headquarters' managers become slightly more complex. Issues such as compatibility of hardware and software computer systems, management information systems, financial reporting systems, strategic planning systems, and human resources management systems all need to be negotiated. After the merger, any of these issues could lead to months of bargaining and disagreements.

Formalization

Conglomerate mergers should lead to minimal changes in the degree of formalization for the acquired unit. Here, management is mostly interested in the quarterly as well as the end-of-the-year financial results. As long as these returns match what the parent firm expected, no major new rules will be issued to the new unit. However, even in the best of circumstances, parent firms slowly and sometimes subconsciously issue new regulations to the new unit. The human resources reporting system is a prime example. Usually, shortly after the merger the acquired unit receives a new human resources reporting system. In order to make sense of the system, a thick manual is also enclosed that details how it can be implemented. Now, to comply with the new system, chances are most of the unit's existing human resources practices need to be modified. Each change requires more training for managers and supervisors as well as updates to inform the employees. A similar scenario can be imagined for the financial reporting system and many other existing systems. Thus, in conglomerate mergers, change is more subtle and slower than in related mergers—but it is change, nonetheless.

Interestingly, if the unit's financial results are deficient in any way, the imposition of new systems by the parent firm becomes more obvious and deliberate. Here, the situation very much resembles that of related mergers. Teams of experts from headquarters may suddenly descend on the division to "fix" its lackluster performance. Sometimes a unit's performance in terms of financial results is on par with its previous performance; yet headquarters may perceive its performance deficient, compared with other businesses in its portfolio. For example, if the acquisition is in the beer industry where growth in revenues may be in the 1 to 2 percent range, and the unit is achieving a 1.5 percent growth in revenues, this return may not be adequate for the corporate office accustomed to a 10 percent growth rate for every business in its portfolio. Thus, headquarters managers may become impatient and attempt to fix a business that—given its industry norms—may not be broken.

Centralization

Similar to vertical and concentric mergers, in conglomerate mergers, executives of the acquiring firm do not necessarily have expertise in each of their acquisitions' industries. So it is wise for them to allow each unit independence and autonomy in decision making to maintain the strategic flexibility of the unit and prevent it from losing its competitive advantage. Thus, centralization should be minimal in order to allow experts in each unit to devise their strategy and operating plans. The financial success of the acquired unit is often one of the main determinants of the degree of autonomy it is allowed: The more successful, the more autonomous.

SUMMARY

Structure is a key tool in implementing the strategies of a corporation. The type of merger that is undertaken partly determines the degree of structural change that the two organizations will undergo (see Figure 4.3). Generally, related mergers lead to the greatest amount of structural change, particularly for the acquired firm. On the other hand, conglomerate mergers usually require limited structural adjustment by the two merger partners. After a merger, the entire structure of a firm needs to be examined to ensure its alignment with the new environment of the organization and its strategy and culture.

Structure's three key dimensions of complexity, formalization, and centralization *will* change after a merger, sometimes very rapidly and at times slowly; yet we find managers surprisingly ill-prepared for these changes. It seems that financial considerations and the consummation of the merger

Figure 4.3
Degree of Structural Change in Each Type of Merger

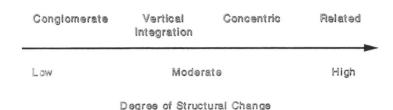

take most of their attention away from organizational issues and rather superficial planning is done for "the day after." Managers of both firms need to recognize that these changes are forthcoming, and they need to *plan* for them. These implementation-related changes can easily derail a well-intentioned merger—or at least postpone its success for many years.

Managers need to view mergers as an opportunity to review all the rules—not just those of the acquired unit. This strategy allows the managers of both firms to engage in healthy debate concerning which rules impede productivity. The goal should be to keep only the minimum number of rules necessary for the efficient operation of the overall business. By allowing employees to suggest changes to those rules that affect them the most and accepting their suggestions, managers start to move the organization forward. Stressing that a merger interlocks the fate of both firms, making turf warfare unacceptable is one of the key strategies used.

NOTES

1. See R. H. Hall, *Organizations: Structures, processes, and outcomes* (Englewood Cliffs, NJ: Prentice-Hall, 1977).

2. Hall, *Organizations*.

3. Hall, *Organizations*.

4. For an excellent study of the length of time it takes to merge in related mergers, see A. F. Buono & J. L. Bowditch, *The human side of mergers and acquisitions* (San Francisco: Jossey-Bass, 1989).

Part II

Acculturation

5

How to Combine Two Organizations

Having a strong culture is seen as a desirable attribute by most organizations. The strength of the culture builds commitment and provides stability. As discussed in Chapter 2, though, that same strength makes change very painful. However, all organizations undergo change, and many of the changes that have taken place during recent years have been the direct or indirect result of mergers and acquisitions. Organizations with different and sometimes totally incompatible cultures have come together, and employees have simply been expected to adapt to each other. However, in light of the role of culture in organizations and the investment that most employees have in it, coming in contact with another culture and being forced to change one's own constitutes a very difficult task. How do people deal with cultural changes? What effect does contact with another culture have on the individual and on the collective identity of a group? How much do individuals change? How much does an organization change? How much of the culture is maintained?

This chapter will provide answers to these questions by defining the concept of acculturation, its stages, and its different modes. The factors that lead to the choice of an acculturation mode for the acquired and the acquiring firm will be presented along with the characteristics of each mode and some basic ideas for managing each.

WHAT IS ACCULTURATION?

Acculturation is the term used to describe the process by which two groups that have come in direct contact resolve the conflicts and problems that inevitably arise as a result of their contact. It is defined as changes that occur in both cultures as a result of the contact.[1] The concept is used extensively in cross-cultural psychology and anthropology to study and explain how indigenous cultures adapt to colonial ones. In this context, the process of acculturation has been studied for many years. Although the process of getting to know and function with another culture can be a highly positive experience, often it is not. Owing to a variety of factors, the most common outcomes are disruption and alienation for members of the less dominant culture and, in some cases, destruction of entire cultures.

Until a few years ago, acculturation was the exclusive domain of anthropologists and cross-cultural psychologists. However, the concept has been found to be applicable to organizational cultures and has come to be used to explain the contact between two cultures in a merger situation.

Stages of Acculturation

In mergers, two independent groups of people who often have very different cultures come in firsthand contact, which takes place in three stages: contact, conflict, and adaptation (see Figure 5.1). There is no set time line for this process. In some cases, conflict is unending; in other cases, adaptation comes quickly and relatively painlessly.

Contact. After the initial courtship and after the merger becomes a legal reality, members of the two organizations come in contact to varying degrees. In some cases, such as in conglomerate mergers, contact is minimal as the two companies become part of a common corporate financial umbrella. In other cases (i.e., in related mergers), extensive need for synergy in various areas forces the employees of the acquirer and the acquired firm to interact closely. The initial contact therefore sets the stage for the relationship between the two groups. The outcome of the relationship will depend on a number of factors ranging from the type of merger to the strength of the two cultures. Regardless of the outcome, the initial contact is likely to engender some level of conflict.

Conflict. As the members of each of the merging firms grapple with the problems of getting to know the other group and working with them, a number of conflicts are bound to arise. When the two firms have little contact and only share a financial umbrella, conflict is likely to be minimal. They do not have to have daily interaction, and they compete for resources only indirectly. One group does not have to give up its prized procedures and norms to adjust to the other. They do not share common management or even common goals and markets. Each firm's strategy can remain relatively independent of the other's. Since the structures of the two organizations do not change drastically, they can coexist relatively peacefully and can treat the parent company almost as an external factor.

As discussed in Chapter 3, the situation is drastically different when the acquirer and the acquired organizations are in similar markets or industries,

Figure 5.1
Stages of Acculturation

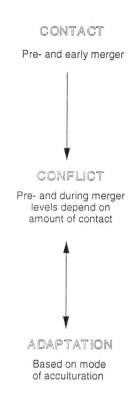

CONTACT

Pre- and early merger

CONFLICT

Pre- and during merger
levels depend on
amount of contact

ADAPTATION

Based on mode
of acculturation

have similar technologies, or are related to each other in some way. The goal of such a merger is to achieve synergy, to some extent, in one or more areas, which will inevitably lead the employees of the two firms to come in close contact. In these cases, conflict is often unavoidable, as both groups vie for power and try to protect their turf and way of life. In most cases, the acquirer imposes various operational and financial controls on the acquired firm. Additionally, pay and benefit systems are often changed, as are management techniques and, most important, management philosophies. The acquired firm may try to impose either an autocratic or a democratic approach to management. Regardless of the direction of the change, it is likely to engender resistance from the members of the acquired organization. Resistance may be passive, as was, for example, the case with many employees of the old Sperry divisions who refused to give up their Sperry ID cards after the merger with Honeywell. However, there may also be open resistance to imposed changes. The stronger the cultures of two firms, the stronger resistance will be to change.

Adaptation. Although dissension may often appear unending, the conflicts related to the contact between two groups are likely to be resolved either positively or negatively. If the conflict is managed well, the two groups can come to an agreement over how synergy is to be achieved—which operational and cultural elements will be preserved and which will be changed. In a positive adaptation, the two groups will agree on how to manage different aspects of their new relationship. With this agreement will come a sense of satisfaction about the relationship and the future. On the other hand, a negative adaptation will involve continuing conflict and lack of agreement over how the merger should be handled. As a result, one group or both groups are likely to feel cheated and will continue to harbor resentment and dissatisfaction. Much of the employee- or company-generated turnover in the acquired firm takes place when adaptation is not achieved quickly or when the outcome does not match the various parties' expectations.

MODES OF ACCULTURATION

The course acculturation takes depends on many different factors. When studying the mergers that have taken place over the last few years, it appears that most acquirers attempt to impose their own procedures and culture on their acquisitions. After all, the acquirer must be doing things better than the company it is acquiring since it can afford to buy it. This sense of superiority further aggravates the conflict since it often occurs in light of premerger promises to respect the acquired firm's independence and culture. The frequent occurrence of events such as these makes it evident that companies, regardless of the type of merger, assume that the only way to handle a merger is for the acquired firm to be assimilated into the parent company—not only in the legal and financial senses but also in regard to its culture. Given the higher number of less-than-successful mergers that have been undertaken, it seems evident that assimilation is by no means the only way or the best way to merge two cultures.

Based on the concept of acculturation, when two cultures come in contact, there are four general ways in which they can interact with each other. Each mode involves a different way of adapting to the contact between two cultures and a method of resolving emerging conflict.

Assimilation

The most common way the conflict between two cultures is resolved is for one of them, most likely the acquired firm, to give up its practices, procedures, and philosophies and become totally assimilated into the acquired firm. In this situation, the members of the acquired firm relinquish their culture and adopt that of the acquirer. In assimilation, the flow of culture is only one way. The acquired firm changes its culture and adopts its acquirer's; the acquirer does not change. Assimilation requires cooperation and acceptance of change from members of the acquired company. Willingness to change is likely to stem from a weak, unsuccessful, or dysfunctional culture. During the contact with the acquirer, members of the acquired firm resolve the conflict by willingly giving up their own identity and taking on that of the acquirer.

Overall, in assimilation, the acquired firm will be absorbed into the acquirer and will cease to exist not only as a legal entity but also as a cultural one. As mentioned earlier, assimilation tends to be one of the most common paths taken during a merger. Frequently, it is expected that the acquired company will cease to exist. The St. Regis and Champion merger is a good example of assimilation, as St. Regis ceased to exist and became an integral part of Champion. The Burroughs (now Honeywell)-Sperry merger also exemplified assimilation, although it was not without resistance.

Integration

A mode of acculturation that is often overlooked as a choice in mergers is integration. As compared with assimilation, integration is less unilateral. In integration, the acquired firm maintains most, if not all, of the cultural and organizational elements that provide it with its unique identity. The desire to maintain culture is related to both its strength and its success. The acquirer allows its acquisition some degree of freedom and independence to maintain its culture even though it has become a legal and financial part of the parent company. As a result, integration leads to structural assimilation but little behavioral and cultural assimilation.

Another characteristic of integration as a mode of acculturation is the sharing of cultural elements. Both firms change some, but not all, of their culture and adopt some elements from the other firm's culture. Contact between the two firms remains cordial, which further allows for, and en courages, exchange of various organizational and cultural elements.

Overall, integration involves a moderate level of conflict as the two organizations openly as well as implicitly negotiate exchanges. Such negotiations were reported to be common during the IBM-Rolm merger. Initially, both companies had agreed that integration was most appropriate. Rolm retained much of the independence it needed to remain an entrepreneurial organization; yet it also became part of IBM by having many of its products used by IBM's divisions. The merger of Denmark's biggest banks in 1990 provides another example of integration.[2] After the merger, everything from dress code to the logo had to be negotiated and was changed for both merger partners.

Separation

Separation as a mode of acculturation involves an attempt by the acquired firm to remain separate from the parent company by retaining all its cultural elements and practices. In separation, members of the acquired organization refuse to assimilate with the acquirer at any level. They have a strong culture that they want to maintain and want to function as a separate entity under the umbrella of the parent company. Separation, therefore, requires minimal contact and exchange between the firms. Because of the desire to remain separate, and the rejection of the parent company's cultural and organizational elements and practices, separation engenders a fair amount of conflict and is likely to be difficult to implement. As is the case with the other two modes of acculturation, agreement on the mode to be used is the key to reduction of conflict. The Shearson–American Express merger a few years ago is a good example. American Express traditionally allowed its acquisitions to remain relatively separate. Shearson's fast-paced culture was highly valued by its employees, who were allowed to keep it totally separate from the more planning-oriented American Express. Separation is likely to be very common in cases where the acquirer is a large corporation providing a financial umbrella for smaller units.

The 1989 merger of Materials Research Corporation (MRC) and Sony USA Inc. has also involved separation.[3] The exchange between the two firms remains almost entirely on a financial basis, as is also the case of the merger between Genentech and Hoffman LaRoche.[4]

Deculturation

The last mode of acculturation is the least positive and least desirable. Deculturation involves the loss of all cultural and managerial characteristics. In deculturation, the acquired firm's culture is likely to be weak—therefore leading its members to relinquish it. At the same time, they are not willing to adopt that of the parent company, and as a result, the acquired firm is likely to disintegrate as a cultural and managerial entity. Deculturation leads to a high degree of conflict as well as to confusion and stress for the members of the acquired organization.

The mismanagement of many mergers has led to deculturation for the employees of the acquired firms. Among the many examples are Continental and Eastern Airlines after they were acquired by Lorenzo's Texas Air, and Revlon after having been taken over by Perelman's Pantry Pride. In both cases, employees experienced considerable anxiety and a deep sense of loss that resulted from the destruction of their organization and their careers. The term *acculturative stress* has been used to describe such

Figure 5.2
Modes of Acculturation and Level of Conflict

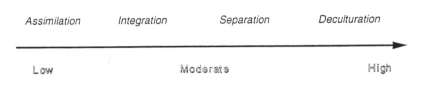

Stages of Acculturation

| Assimilation | Integration | Separation | Deculturation |

Low   Moderate   High

Level of Conflict

experiences.[5] It refers to stress that results from the negative resolution of the conflict generated by the contact between two cultures.

Acculturation Modes and Conflict

Each of the modes of acculturation leads to some degree of conflict. Assimilation would engender the least amount of conflict, whereas deculturation leads to the highest level (see Figure 5.2). Integration and separation each lead to a moderate to high level of conflict. The conflict can be positive if managed properly and held at constructive levels. The key in the case of acculturation is discussion of and agreement over which mode of acculturation should be implemented. Such a discussion is possible only if both organizations are aware of their preferred, as well as the most appropriate, modes for their particular situation.

CHOICE OF ACCULTURATION MODES FOR THE ACQUIRED FIRM

The choice of the mode of acculturation for the acquired firm will depend (1) on the strength and success of its own culture and on how much its employees and managers want to preserve it and (2) on the perception of the acquirer (see Figure 5.3).

Strength of Culture

If an organization has a very thick culture with many employees sharing strong, well-defined values and assumptions, it is unlikely that it will be willing to give up its culture or even change it in any substantial way. On the other hand, if members of an organization do not share common cultural elements, assumptions and values are unclear and poorly ordered, or employees feel that such elements have not been conducive to success, they are likely to be willing to change their culture or even adopt a new

Figure 5.3
Acculturation Modes for the Acquired Firm

STRENGTH OF CULTURE

	Weak	Strong
High	Assimilation	Integration
Low	Deculturation	Separation

ATTRACTION
TO
ACQUIRER

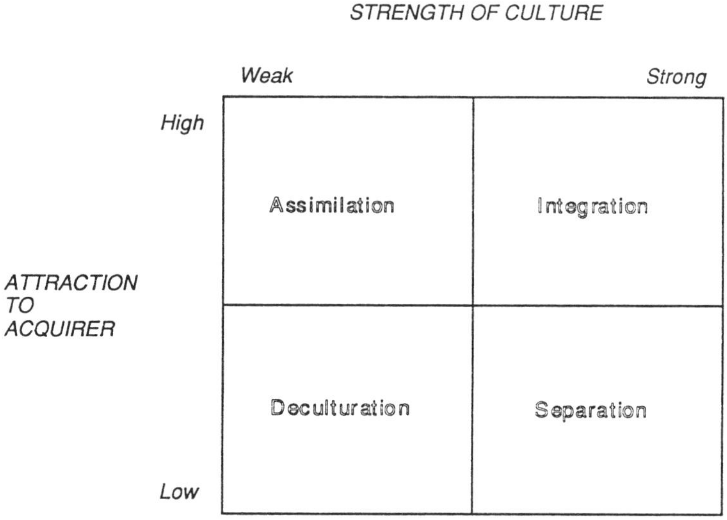

one. In the case of a strong, thick culture, integration and separation
become the most likely modes of acculturation. In both of these modes,
members of an organization keep their cultural and managerial elements
and other characteristics that make them unique. On the other hand, if
the culture is weak and thin, assimilation is the most likely mode and would
involve a large-scale cultural change. Deculturation is also likely to result
if the culture is weak or if it is weakened.

Perception of Attractiveness of the Acquirer

The second factor that determines the choice of acculturation modes for
the acquired firm is the degree to which they perceive the acquirer as
attractive. In other words, to what extent do members of the acquired firm
admire and value the culture, managerial style and philosophy, and performance of the acquirer? If the perception of the acquired firm is positive
and members of the acquired organization are attracted to the acquirer,
they are likely to seek either integration or assimilation as a mode of
acculturation. Integration would allow for some cultural exchange as long
as it is balanced; assimilation would involve total cultural absorption. On
the other hand, if members of the acquired firm perceive the acquirer as
unworthy and unattractive, they are likely to reject any cultural exchange
and therefore attempt to remain separate.

The choice of acculturation becomes clear when the two factors are
combined (see Figure 5.3). An acquired firm is likely to prefer integration

Figure 5.4
Acculturation Modes for the Acquirer

CULTURE

	Unicultural	Multicultural
Related	Assimilation	Integration
Unrelated	Deculturation	Separation

STRATEGY

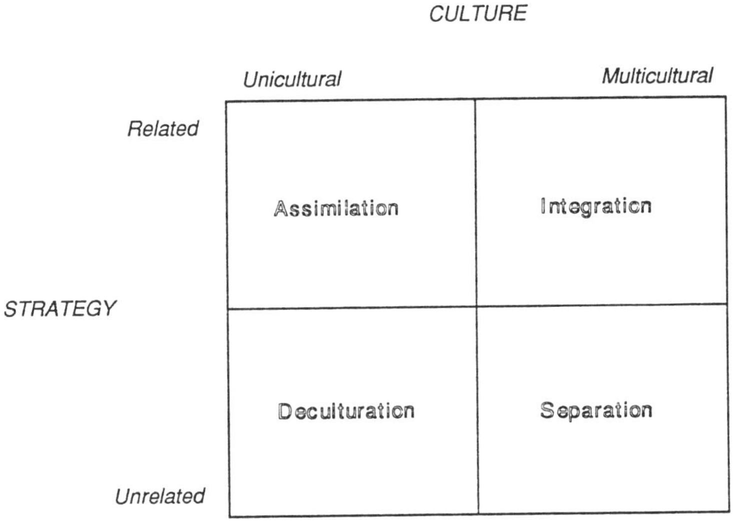

if members want to preserve their own culture and identity but at the same time find the acquirer worthy and attractive enough to want to exchange cultural and managerial elements with it. Assimilation will be the preferred mode of acculturation when members of the acquired firm do not value their own culture but find the acquirer attractive and are therefore willing to adopt its culture. Separation will be appropriate when an acquired company's culture is strong and thick and the acquirer is not perceived as attractive. The least desirable case is deculturation, whereby members of the acquired firm do not want to maintain their own culture, do not find the acquirer attractive, and therefore reject both cultures.

CHOICE OF ACCULTURATION MODES FOR THE ACQUIRER

From the point of view of the acquirer, which mode of acculturation is selected and which is appropriate depend on its strategy and on its culture. The combination of the two factors determines which mode of acculturation should be implemented (see Figure 5.4).

Role of Strategy in Acculturation

One of the factors that determines how an acquisition will be managed is the strategy of the acquirer. The strategy will partly determine how a new acquisition will be managed. If, for example, the goal of the merger is to achieve synergy in the financial, operational, and managerial levels, it will be managed differently than if the goal of the merger is only financial integration. In the first case, as discussed earlier, an acquirer is likely to get involved with its acquisition and attempt to make many changes in order to create the synergies it seeks. In the case of a corporation that simply provides a financial umbrella, the likelihood of much interference with the acquired firm is not as high.

Overall, the diversification strategy of a firm will influence the mode of acculturation sought. If the merger is with a firm in a relatively related business (related or concentric merger), the acquirer is more likely to impose some or all of its culture and practices in an attempt to achieve operating synergies. On the other hand, an acquirer is less likely to interfere with the culture and practices of a relatively unrelated acquisition (vertical or conglomerate merger).[6] Therefore, when acquiring somewhat related firms, an acquirer is much more likely to prefer either integration or assimilation as the mode of acculturation. These two modes involve considerable exchange of cultural and managerial elements between the two organizations. In the case of assimilation, the acquirer will impose all of its practices on its acquisition. On the other hand, when merging with only partially or totally unrelated firms, the more appropriate mode of acculturation is separation. Since the two firms are unrelated, the acquirer does not have specific expertise in the management, operations, or technology of its acquisitions. Therefore, it would be more appropriate for the acquisition to be given a high degree of autonomy and independence. Such autonomy would be possible if it is allowed to remain separate from its parent company (see Figure 5.4).

Role of the Acquirer's Culture in Acculturation

The second element that determines the appropriate mode of acculturation from the point of view of the acquirer is the culture of the organization. The key factor is the degree to which the acquirer is multicultural. *Multiculturalism*, in this context, refers to the degree to which an organization values organizational cultural diversity and is willing to tolerate and encourage it. If an organization simply contains many different cultural groups (as many large, diverse organizations do), it can be considered to be a plural organization. If in addition to including several cultures, the organization values this diversity and nurtures and encourages it, it is considered to be multicultural. A multicultural acquirer is likely to consider diversity an asset and consequently allow the acquired firm to retain its own culture and practices. On the other hand, a unicultural acquirer will emphasize conformity and reward adherence to unique goals, strategies, and managerial and organizational practices. Consequently, it is more likely to impose its own culture and management systems on a new acquisition.

Integration is the most likely mode when the two businesses are totally or partially related and the acquirer is multicultural. The acquisition will be allowed to maintain some autonomy and much of its culture, while at the same time there will be attempts at achieving synergy in several areas. Assimilation will occur when the two businesses are relatively related and the acquirer is unicultural and will not tolerate diversity. The acquirer is likely to have enough expertise about some aspects of its acquisition to allow it to impose its culture and managerial practices. When the two businesses are relatively unrelated and the acquirer is multicultural, separation becomes the most appropriate mode of acculturation. The acquisition is allowed to function relatively autonomously, given that the acquirer has little expertise in the latter's business. Deculturation is the most likely mode of acculturation when the businesses are somewhat unrelated but the unicultural nature of the acquirer leads it to interfere in the operations and management of its acquisition, thereby generating high levels of conflict and stress (see Figure 5.4). A review of the outcomes of many mergers indicates that deculturation is unusually common. To a large extent, the frequent occurrence is due to the total lack of sensitivity to organizational culture and acculturation factors.

The course of the acculturation process depends on the preferences of the two companies involved in the merger. If the two organizations agree on how they should be combined, there will be minimal conflict. If they disagree, however, the conflict that will likely result will detract from organizational performance and will impede the success of the merger for many years.

CHARACTERISTICS OF EACH ACCULTURATION MODE

Each of the four modes of acculturation presents different characteristics in terms of risk, control, and cultural and structural change. These characteristics will often be different from the vantages of the acquirer and the acquired organization. Table 5.1 presents the characteristics of each of the modes for both partners.

Assimilation

Acquirer. From the point of view of the acquirer, assimilation appears to be the easiest mode. The acquired firm simply becomes part of the parent company culturally, structurally, and financially. The risk is relatively low since there is maximum control over the new partner. In addition, the acquirer has to undergo very minimal cultural changes because there is no cultural exchange in assimilation. The acquirer does not have to change much of its structure either. Closely related departments are absorbed by their counterparts in the existing structure; others are either disbanded or transformed to fit an established division. As a result, there

Table 5.1
Characteristics of Acculturation Modes for the Acquirer and the Acquired Firm

		DEGREE OF RISK	DEGREE OF CONTROL	CULTURAL CHANGES	STRUCTURAL CHANGES
INTEGRATION	A:	moderate	moderate	some	some
	B:	moderate	moderate	some	some
ASSIMILATION	A:	low	high	none	minimal
	B:	high	low	total	total
SEPARATION	A:	high	low	none	minimal
	B:	low	high	none	minimal
DECULTURATION	A:	none	high	none	none
	B:	very high	very low	total	total

A: From the point of view of the acquirer
B : From the point of view of the acquired firm

are only minor adjustments in reporting relationships. The degree of centralization does not have to change. The acquisition will become as formal as the parent company. The only structural factor that is affected to some degree is complexity with the addition of new division employees within the existing divisions. Assuming that there are no layoffs, the increase in size alone will add to the complexity.

The initial low risk and high control of assimilation for the acquirer is often offset by the considerable difficulty in implementation. The problems are due to the resistance of the acquired firm to "simply become part" of the acquirer. For the acquired firm, assimilation may be one of the hardest modes, especially if it was not a preference in the first place.

Acquired Firm. In order to assimilate with the acquirer, members of an acquired organization have to give up their culture. Even if they do so willingly, assimilation involves a high degree of risk, since they are unlikely to have in-depth knowledge of their partner's culture. They are entering unchartered waters. In addition, the acquired organization is giving up control over its fate to its partner. Since it will cease to exist as a separate entity either culturally or legally, it is also likely to undergo considerable structural change. Its departments might be broken apart, or reporting relationships might change. Work routines might be modified, and new rules and policies might be applied, leading to more or less formalization. All these factors lead assimilation to entail considerable adjustment for the acquired firm. These adjustments become particularly difficult if the members of the organization did not select assimilation as their preferred mode.

Integration

Given the balanced nature of integration, the merger partners are likely to face relatively similar situations. Integration leads to changes in both organizations. Both have to accept some risk as they open up to the other, and both will lose some control over their culture and organization. At the same time, they will gain some control over the other firm. They will be exchanging cultural elements; therefore, both will undergo some degree of cultural change. The structure of both is likely to change as they wrestle with trying to create a new whole out of two organizations that will, at the same time, remain separate. Overall, integration involves not only a somewhat balanced exchange of culture; it also involves balanced difficulties for the two organizations. They will both undergo some reorganization and adjustment.

Separation

Acquirer. Separation is a very high risk endeavor for the acquirer. The autonomy given the acquisition will lead to high risk and little control. The acquisition will be allowed to "do its own thing." If successful, the risk will appear low; however, the acquired firm's mistakes can jeopardize the acquirer without the latter having immediate control. Separation will require minimal cultural change for the acquirer. Structurally, the change will come only at a corporate level with the addition of a new division and therefore will not cause adjustments in the reporting relationships on a day-to-day basis.

Acquired Firm. Whereas assimilation appeared to be the easiest mode for the acquirer, separation may be the easiest for the acquired firm. Members get to maintain their culture and practices and function autonomously. From the point of view of the acquired firm, the risk is low, since it can maintain high control over its own destiny. There are minimal cultural or structural changes, and employees are likely to experience very few changes in their day-to-day operations and activities, especially in the short run.

Deculturation

Deculturation involves almost no changes for the acquirer. The acquired firm, however, will experience total loss of control and destruction of its culture. It is, therefore, a highly risky situation for one of the partners. Deculturation is a very unlikely prospect for the members of the acquiring organization. The possibility of losing their culture as a result of a merger is very remote. The acquirer, however, may cause deculturation in their acquisition either intentionally or accidentally. In situations where the goal of the merger is to cut up the acquisition and sell off its various parts to different buyers, deculturation will occur. On the other hand, deculturation might result unintentionally, as a result of forcing an unwanted mode of acculturation on the merger partner.

MANAGING THE ACCULTURATION PROCESS

No One Best Way

The review of the many mergers that have taken place over the past ten years indicates that acquirers often attempt to get their new acquisition to assimilate to their culture. It appears that managers make the incorrect assumption that assimilation is the best approach since it will "bring in" the new group and make them part of the parent company. This is often done over the protest and active resistance of the members of the acquired firm. Furthermore, managers of acquiring firms often fail to consider their own goals and culture. If the goal of the merger is financial synergy and the two businesses are not related, what purpose would be served by assimilating the acquired firm into the acquiring organization? Neither the goal of the merger nor the nature of the two businesses requires such action. In such situations, separation would be the most appropriate mode of acculturation. However, allowing an acquisition to retain its autonomy requires high tolerance for diversity and a multicultural organization, characteristics that are not found frequently in many firms.

Another situation would arise in a merger with a related firm. In such a case, the goal of the merger is likely to be operational, technological, and/or managerial synergy, which require more extensive contact and exchange between the two companies. Depending on the degree of multiculturalism of the acquirer, integration or assimilation can be implemented. A multicultural acquirer will allow more autonomy to its acquisition, whereas a unicultural one is likely to require adoption of common goals and practices. It is essential for an acquirer to pursue strategies that are congruent with its culture. For example, unrelated acquisitions may be very difficult to manage and to implement for unicultural acquirers.

There is, therefore, no one best way to manage the acculturation process. The success of the acculturation process depends on knowledge of both organizational cultures and awareness of the goal and type of merger in order to create the cultural and managerial environment needed for its success.

Agreement on the Mode of Acculturation

Each party in a merger is likely to have different goals regarding both the process and the outcome of the merger. The acquirer and the acquired firms are likely to have different preferences regarding the way mergers are managed and which mode of acculturation is used for the implementation of the merger. Although the acquirer may have the power to impose its preference on its new acquisition, such actions are likely to create both resistance and resentment, which are not conducive to long-term success and productivity. Therefore, sincere efforts should be made to negotiate which mode of acculturation would be appropriate, and the two parties should agree on which mode will be implemented. If the two organizations agree on the mode of acculturation, the conflict that results from the contact between them will be positively resolved. Such agreement does not require the cultures and practices of the two organizations to be similar.

The Paths of Least Resistance and the Dynamic Nature of Acculturation

Changing the Acquired Firm. Disagreements over the acculturation process can be more or less manageable, depending on the factors that cause them. When such disagreements occur, successful management of the acculturation process involves attempting to move one or both organizations to a different mode where congruence and agreement are likely to occur. Figure 5.5 presents the possible changes in acculturation preferences. For both the acquirer and the acquired firm, vertical and horizontal movements are easier than diagonal movements, since the latter involve considerably more change of attitude or strategy. For instance, an acquirer may be able to convince its new acquisition to move from separation to integration by pointing out the high success and productivity it has had and demonstrating the attractiveness of its culture and the benefits that it has brought its employees and other constituents. For example, the Shearson–American Express merger started as a separation, but soon both firms found many common themes and moved to integration. However, it would be considerably more difficult to move that same acquisition from separation to

Figure 5.5
Changing Acculturation Modes

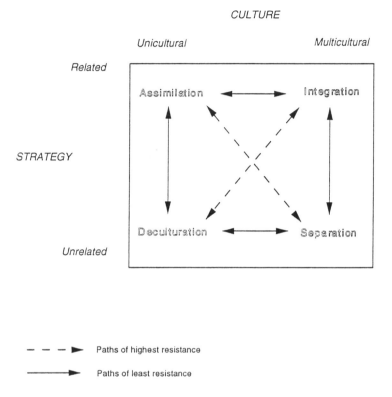

CULTURE

Unicultural   Multicultural

Related

Assimilation ⟷ Integration

STRATEGY

Deculturation ⟷ Separation

Unrelated

— — — ▶   Paths of highest resistance

————————▶   Paths of least resistance

assimilation. Such a move would require the acquired organization to accept not only that the acquirer is attractive and worthy but also that its own culture and practices are not. Such a change would be very difficult and highly unlikely. If assimilation is forced, the outcome might even be deculturation.

A company is acquired because it is considered a valuable and desirable asset. To a great extent, that value comes from its culture, its employees, and its business practices. If the organization is forced to acculturate through a mode that members have not agreed to, the possible deculturation that results would engender the destruction of that culture and alienation of its members. Such an outcome cannot lead to long-term profitability. The cultural destruction may, of course, be irrelevant in cases where the goal of the acquirer is to break down the acquired company's assets and sell them off. Such actions are not oriented toward long-term profitability and therefore do not involve any attempts at acculturation and management; as a result, they are not related to the topics of discussion in this book.

Although successful management of the acculturation process does not require similarity of cultures, it does require for the two firms to have some common grounds and understanding for each other. A further challenge in the management of acculturation is the fact that although there may be initial agreement on the mode, contact between the two groups may lead to changes in employees' preferences for the mode of acculturation. For example, a white knight that may have been viewed very positively by members of an organization may upon closer examination and further contact appear highly undesirable. Initial promises of independence and autonomy may not be fulfilled once the merger becomes a reality. These events may move the acquired firm from preference for integration or even assimilation to desire to remain separate.

Alternately, further knowledge and contact with the managers and employees of a parent company may create a more positive image for the acquired firm. The example of the MRC and Sony merger presented earlier in this chapter is a case in point. The initial separation of the two under Sony's corporate umbrella is slowly being changed by some technological exchanges between the two firms.

Changing the Acquirer. Just as the perception and attitude of an acquired firm's employees may change as a result of contact with the parent company, an acquirer may also change as a consequence of its experience with mergers or contact with a particular target firm. For example, a corporation that is becoming highly diversified may become more multicultural as a result of the development of many different cultures within it. Consequently, although initially it encouraged assimilation of all acquisitions, it may, with time, allow for integration of some and separation of others. Overall, acculturation is not a one-time, static choice made by members of two organizations. It is highly dynamic and requires careful monitoring and periodic adjustment and renegotiation.

SUMMARY

When two organizations come in contact during a merger, there are four general ways in which their conflicts can be resolved. These four modes of acculturation are ways that the two companies' cultures can be merged. The first mode is assimilation, which involves one organization's being totally absorbed into the other. One culture disappears as the two firms merge. The second mode, integration, is a more balanced process whereby both cultures are retained while there is much interaction and exchange of cultures. Separation, the third mode, leads to the two firms' remaining totally separate and sharing only a financial or legal umbrella. In this case, there is no exchange of culture. The last and least desirable mode of acculturation is deculturation, a mode that involves the destruction of one or both cultures as a result of high unresolved conflict.

Although assimilation seems to be the common expectation during a merger, integration and separation are also viable ways to resolve conflict. The choice of the mode of acculturation depends on the preferences of the firms involved. For the acquired organization, the choice of acculturation is determined by the strength of its culture and the degree to which the acquirer is perceived to be attractive. For the acquirer, the choice of mode depends on the strategy of the firm and the degree to which it is multicultural. Positive acculturation does not require similarity between the cultures of the two firms. Instead, it hinges on agreement on the mode of acculturation to be used in the implementation of the merger.

Each of the modes of acculturation has particular characteristics in terms of degree of risk and control, and cultural and structural change. The same mode is different depending on whether it is viewed from the point of view of the acquirer or the acquired firm. Planning the cultural aspects of merger through particularly proactive planning of the acculturation process is essential in successful resolution of the conflict that results from the contact of two organizations in a merger. First, the acquirer needs to be aware of and understand its own culture and strategy; and second, it must be cognizant of its target goals and desires. Changes of preference are to be expected over time. Although forcing a mode on the merger partner cannot lead to long-term performance, negotiation to change the preferred mode can.

NOTES

1. For detailed discussion of acculturation in cross-cultural psychology, see J. W. Berry, 1980; Social and cultural change, in H. C. Triandis & R. W. Brislin (Eds.), *Handbook of cross-cultural psychology*, Vol. 5, pp. 211–279. (Boston: Allyn & Bacon, 1980); J. W. Berry, Acculturation: A comparative analysis of alternative forms, in R. J. Samuda & S. L. Woods (Eds.), *Perspectives in immigrant and minority education*, pp. 11–270 (Orlando, FL: Academic Press, 1983).

2. G. Evans, Denmark: Pinstripes versus the Trinity, *Euromoney*, February 1991, pp. 63–66.

3. R. Whiting, Material Research gets a new lease on life, *Electronic Business*, 4 February 1991, pp 34–36.

4. I. Picker, H. D. Shapiro, G. VonWyss, L. Conger, & R. Karp, Mergers and acquisitions: Strategic is the word, *Institutional Investor*, 25, no. 1, (1991) pp. 74–81.

5. For a discussion of acculturative stress, see J. W. Berry, & R. C. Annis, Acculturative stress: The role of ecology, culture and differentiation, *Journal of Cross-Cultural Psychology*, 5 (1974), pp. 382–406.

6. See G. M. Walter, Culture collision in mergers and acquisitions, in P. J. Frost, L. F. Moore, M. R. Louis, C. C. Lundberg, & J. Martin (Eds.), *Organizational culture*, pp. 301–314 (Beverly Hills, CA: Sage, 1985).

6

Leadership

It is commonly agreed that leaders have tremendous influence on their organizations. The focus on top managers in the popular business press is an indication of the importance we give leaders. Top executives and business owners are our national heroes. Organizations that are undergoing major changes invariably replace their top managers. Likewise, organizations that do not perform up to expectations often change top managers. The astronomical salaries given some top executives reflect their worth to the organization. Obviously, leaders are one of the most important elements in organizations, and in the United States, as well as many other nations, this high regard for leadership approaches awe.

Much has been written about the ways in which leaders influence organizations. Leaders are one of the major sources of culture (see Chapter 2). They create structures and set strategies; therefore, they are very influential.

Mergers, however, present even more of a challenge for leadership. During a merger "all bets are off." All the practices and traditions that an organization has come to rely on are questioned, if not discarded; so mergers lead to considerable change and uncertainty. This is particularly the case for members of the acquired firm.

The overreliance on leaders during a merger provides an explanation for the strong sense of betrayal experienced by employees and managers when their leaders "bail out" with a variety of golden parachutes. After all, leaders are the ones who negotiate the merger. They make the final decisions on the mode of acculturation, and they guide the organization through the stages of the conflict. They are symbols of the organization, and they come to be symbols of the merger.

This chapter focuses on the role of the leader in mergers. First, the reasons for the leader's influence will be presented. Second, the relevant leader personal characteristics and their impact on the choice of acculturation modes will be perused. Finally, the role of leadership in helping manage uncertainty and anxiety during mergers will be discussed.

IMPACT OF UNCERTAINTY

The inordinate focus on the roles and effects of leaders comes in the face of somewhat contradictory research findings. In opposition to the popular press, academic research has found the leader to have varying degrees of impact on the organization.[1] In some cases, leaders are assumed and found to have considerable discretion and impact on the organization; in other cases, the leader's role is found to be negligible. Although contradictory findings exist, it has been found that the leader has impact in some circumstances more than others.[2] In times of crisis, particularly, the need for leadership increases.

Uncertainty from Outside

The leader has been found to have impact when the organization is still young and small, when it is in decline, and in times of external and internal turbulence and uncertainty. When the environment is uncertain, decisions are not bound by well-established procedures. The past does not provide easy answers to future decisions because the future is uncertain. The uncertainty may come from a highly competitive industry, economic factors, or any other external factors. No matter what the cause, external uncertainty gives the leader more power to impact the organization. For example, when decisions regarding competitors are routine, because there are few competitors and they are well known, an organization can rely on its past success in making a decision for the future. However, when the environment becomes uncertain with a new competitor entering the field, the CEO or the whole top management team (TMT) are likely to be heavily involved in the strategic decision making regarding how to deal with the newcomer.

Uncertainty from Inside

When there are many successful, well-established patterns of behavior and decision making, as would be the case when an organization has a strong culture, the leader's impact tends to decrease.[3] A strong culture acts as a substitute for leadership by providing behavioral norms, and decisional standards that are usually provided by a leader. High internal uncertainty, on the other hand, provides a leader with the opportunity to influence the organization. For example, in a young organization where new departments are being formed, a conflict regarding jurisdiction is likely to end up on the CEO's desk, as there are no previous patterns to rely on. In organizations that are mature, however, relationships between departments tend to be well established. Interactions are regulated by precedence, and if conflict arises, it is likely to be handled through previously tested mechanisms; only crisis situations would require higher-level intervention.

Uncertainty during Mergers

Mergers tend to create a state of crisis, which provides for an increase in the leader's influence. During a merger, from the most microlevel to the most strategic, aspects of an organization are challenged. Dress code and norms for relationships are examined. Reporting relationships and management practices are challenged, and assumptions are questioned. Job titles are changed, company logos are replaced, and retirement plans are modified to match those of the merger partner. Work forces are "right-sized" or "delayered." All these internal changes, along with many more, create a whirlwind of change that shakes an organization's cultural core. All existing practices become suspect and therefore cannot be relied on. Consequently, leaders are much in demand by the employees. These major changes are most likely to occur in the acquired firm. Their having been purchased is in and of itself taken as a weakness, thus justifying changing many of their practices.

The external environment is also likely to change. If the two firms are from the same industry, they each may deal with new clients and suppliers. If they are from different industries, they will have to learn a whole new world that may include new markets and new technologies. In either case, they have to navigate in a highly uncertain external environment at a time when internal cultures and structures are unstable. Such extreme uncertainty creates dependency on leadership, which explains the frequent changes of leadership that accompany mergers. The leaders are expected to provide the guidance and stability that were previously the result of internal and external calm. Therefore, leadership becomes a vital link in the management of a merger.

ROLE OF LEADER'S PERSONAL CHARACTERISTICS IN DETERMINING STRATEGIC CHOICES

Much research has been aimed at trying to identify the relevant personal characteristics of leaders that have the potential to impact strategic decision making. Much of it is disjointed and difficult to apply to strategy. A number of different demographic and psychological variables have been explored. For example, older CEOs have been found to be more risk averse, and those who are insiders attempt to maintain the status quo and are therefore less likely to make changes.[4] Other researchers have considered the impact of a CEO's functional background on an organization's strategic choices.[5]

There is also a considerable body of research that has focused on various personality characteristics. Among the most common is the use of Locus of Control, which indicates the degree to which an individual feels that he or she has control of life and events around him or her.[6] Managers who feel they have control have been found to emphasize R&D and frequent product changes and to tend to be more innovative. The Myers-Briggs Type Indicator (MBTI) has also been used in predicting CEO decision making. For example, it has been suggested that different types of personalities perceive risk differently and therefore select different strategies. Most of the leaders' personal characteristics studied have been found to affect organizational decision making, although the effect is not always very strong. Overall, organizations come, at least to some extent, to reflect their leader's personality and background.

Strategic Types

In spite of the differences in the concepts used to identify leader characteristics, there are two broad themes that run through them. The first theme is the degree to which an individual seeks challenge and is a risk taker—the extent to which a leader exhibits openness to change and innovation. Individuals who are challenge seekers generally feel comfortable with change and are likely to be entrepreneurial. They are likely to attempt high-risk and innovative strategies and feel comfortable with challenging and changing organization practices. On the other hand, individuals who are challenge averse are not comfortable with change and are likely to try to maintain the status quo. As a result, the strategies they select will be more conservative, requiring only minimal change in the organization.

The second theme present in research about CEO characteristics is the leader's need for control and refers to how willing the leader is to give up control—namely, how willing he or she is to delegate authority and allow others to participate in decisions. Individuals who have a high need for control are likely to create a culture that encourages conformity. Decision making will be centralized, and the structure will provide the leader with control over all aspects of the organization. Centralization is at the expense of employee participation and attention to process, and focus is on outcomes. Furthermore, such a culture is likely to have little tolerance for diversity (not only ethnic but also in terms of managerial practices). At the other extreme, individuals with a low need for control will allow others to make decisions and will be comfortable with delegation. The culture of their organization is likely to be more open and flexible, with the leader having low need for control. Such a culture, in turn, is likely to encourage

Figure 6.1
Strategic Leadership Types

NEED FOR CONTROL

	High	Low
High	**HIGH-CONTROL INNOVATOR** Low delegation High innovation Centralized decision making Tight control but adaptable culture	**PARTICIPATIVE INNOVATOR** High delegation High innovation Decentralized decision making Open and adaptable culture
CHALLENGE SEEKING	**STATUS QUO GUARDIAN** Low delegation Low innovation Centralized decision making Tight control and conservative culture	**PROCESS MANAGER** High delegation Low Innovation Decentralized decision making Open but conservative culture
Low		

employee involvement and tolerance for diversity. Figure 6.1 summarizes these four types.

The leader's challenge seeking and need for control will impact his or her decision-making and managerial styles. In the case of merger, the leader's influence will be manifested in two ways. First, the leader is one of the primary decision makers in the choice of strategy that leads to a merger. Second, the leader plays a crucial role in the implementation of a merger, both through the choice of an acculturation mode and in the implementation of that mode.

ROLE OF ACQUIRER LEADER'S PERSONAL CHARACTERISTICS

Choice of Strategy: Formulation

The challenge-seeking dimension presented above represents risk taking and innovation and is most relevant in the way a leader formulates strategy. For example, one leader might pursue a highly risky product and design a strategy that will help produce and market such a product by accepting that there is a high failure risk. Relating back to the strategic dimensions presented in Chapter 2, the leader's strategic type can be used to predict his or her decisions regarding strategy. Challenge-seeking leaders are likely to select strategies that are high risk and innovative. Overall, the innovators (high control and participative) are more apt to select high-risk strategies, whereas the status quo guardians and process managers will select more conservative approaches.

Challenge seeking also manifests itself in the choice of merger types. As presented in Chapter 2, the more related the merger, the less risk involved, since there is expertise within the organization about that business and its industry. Therefore, a related merger is less risky than vertical or conglomerate mergers where the acquired firm does not necessarily have any in-depth knowledge about the acquired unit's business and industry. The latter involve more risk because they cause a firm to move away from familiar territory. Conglomerates have also been found to be the least profitable types of mergers, a factor that further adds to their riskiness.[7] This same risk will attract the challenge-seeking, innovator CEOs. The CEOs who are less attracted to risk will, on the other hand, pursue related mergers where they are more likely to feel at ease.

Implementation of Strategy: Implementation through Acculturation

The success of a selected strategy depends on its proper implementation. The need for control will be one of the major determinants of the leader's preference for the way strategy is implemented. In the case of a merger, one of the keys to implementation is the acculturation process. The leader's preference for acculturation is likely to be one of the determinants of which mode will be selected by both firms in the implementation of the merger. The leader's choice of mode will match his or her type. As described in Chapter 5, each of the modes has special characteristics, and each provides the acquired with different amounts of control and requires different amounts of change (see Figure 6.2).

For the acquirer, assimilation is the least risky approach, since it requires little change and provides for high control. The acquired firm simply becomes part of the parent company. Assimilation is neither risky nor difficult from the point of view of the acquirer, for it is the acquired firm that has to undergo major transformation. Integration, on the other hand, requires the acquirer as well as the acquired firm to change to some extent, since it involves a give and take and an exchange of cultures. In addition, the acquired firm requires some degree of cultural and operating autonomy, which reduce the control of the parent company. All these factors make integration risky and difficult for the acquirer. Whereas assimilation provides full control and little disruption for the acquirer, integration is more complicated.

As compared with the other two modes, separation requires limited contact between the two firms, so it requires very few adjustments in the

Figure 6.2
Degree of Risk and Control for the Acquirer

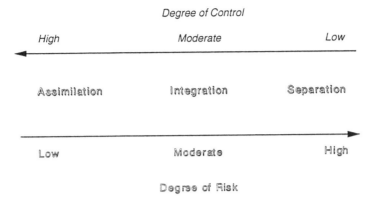

Degree of Control

High   Moderate   Low

Assimilation   Integration   Separation

Low   Moderate   High

Degree of Risk

culture of either firm. However, for separation to work, the acquirer has to give up considerable control over the new acquisition. The acquisition is allowed a high degree of independence and autonomy both culturally and operationally. This factor makes separation very risky from the point of view of the acquirer. The last mode, deculturation, is very unlikely to occur for the acquirer during a merger. It is, however, a possibility for the acquired firm and therefore, it will be discussed in the next section.

Strategic Types and Choice of Acculturation. Figure 6.3 presents the preferences for acculturation based on a leader's strategic type—need for control and, to some extent, need for challenge. As the need for control is the primary dimension for implementation of strategy, it becomes most relevant when considering the choice of acculturation. Each leader has one or more preferences and one or more modes that he or she would consider unsuitable. The high need for control precludes tolerance for, and encouragement of, multiculturalism. The higher the need for control, the more likely that the leader will try to enforce uniform culture, procedures, and practices. The high-control innovator (HCI) is challenge seeking but also needs control over the organization and is likely to find the needed challenge in assimilation and integration. Managing such modes is demanding and requires skillful leadership. However, both modes, particularly assimilation, still provide the leader of the acquiring firm with control over the process. For example, in integration the exchange of culture makes the mode interesting for an HCI. His or her organization is likely to find new ways of doing things; but at the same time, the new acquisition remains close enough to satisfy the leader's need for control.

The HCI will be the least comfortable with separation as a mode for the implementation of a merger. Separation would involve allowing near-total autonomy to the acquisition, and this would go against the HCI's high

Figure 6.3
Preferred Mode of Acculturation for the Leader of the Acquiring Firm

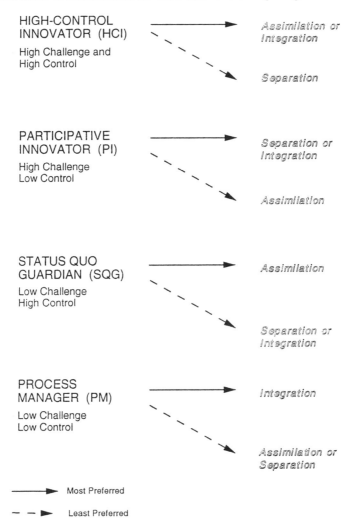

need for control. Harold Geneen of ITT is a good example of an HCI. Geneen is viewed by many as the father of conglomerate mergers. He acquired highly diverse companies, a strategy that was highly innovative and risky. He also maintained a very close watch on his acquisitions through his highly confrontative and control-oriented management style.

Like the HCI, the participative innovator (PI) is a risk taker; however, he or she has a low need for control. The PI is, therefore, likely to be most comfortable with either separation or integration. Both modes require limited control and allow for multiculturalism, since they involve autonomy for the acquirer. They are also challenging, as they involve finding less direct means of maintaining control. On the other hand, assimilation may be very difficult for a PI to handle because it involves close control. Close control would require centralized decision making and low delegation, both of which are apt to make the PI uneasy.

The status quo guardian (SQG) is not a risk taker and has a high need for control, characteristics that would make assimilation the only suitable mode, since it provides for tight control and uniformity. Neither integration nor separation would allow enough involvement in the management of the acquisition. These two modes either would require too much change within the organization or would involve giving the acquisition too much autonomy. Furthermore, the SQG's need for conformity would also be threatened, as integration and separation allow retention of cultural and managerial identity. Integration is more likely to be selected by the process manager (PM), who is risk averse with a low need for control. He or she is therefore likely to be most comfortable with modes that require less control than assimilation and are less risky than separation.

ROLE OF ACQUIRED FIRM'S LEADER'S PERSONAL CHARACTERISTICS IN DETERMINING ACCULTURATION MODES

As is the case with the acquirer, the personal characteristics of the leader of the acquired organization will affect the choice of acculturation. It can even be argued that since the acquired firm is likely to experience a sense of crisis, the leader will have an even greater role than in other, less turbulent times. For the acquired firm, the choice of acculturation may present different characteristics (see Figure 6.4). Whereas for the acquirer assimilation provided the highest control and the lowest risk, the opposite is true for the acquired firm. For the acquired firm, assimilation leads to the highest loss of culture and the highest amount of change—therefore, the highest risk. Taking on a new and unknown culture is particularly difficult. Separation, on the other hand, allows them to keep control of their fate and thus presents relatively low risk. Additionally, although deculturation is not a conscious choice for the acquirer, it is a looming possibility for the members of the acquired firm.

The different goals for the acquired and the acquirer cause leaders with the same styles to prefer different acculturation modes.

Strategic Types and Choice of Acculturation. Figure 6.5 presents the preferences for acculturation based on a leader's strategic type. The HCI's need for control is likely to make him or her most comfortable with separation or integration. Both modes will allow the HCI to maintain authority and influence over the organization while at the same time providing for sufficient challenge. Whereas an HCI in an acquiring firm is likely to select

Figure 6.4
Degree of Risk and Control for the Acquired Firm

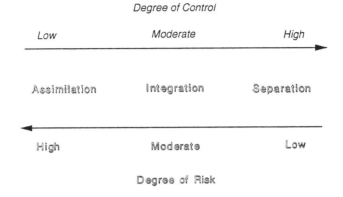

Degree of Control

Low	Moderate	High

Assimilation   Integration   Separation

High   Moderate   Low

Degree of Risk

assimilation and avoid separation, the HCI in an acquired organization
will prefer separation and avoid assimilation. Assimilation for the acquired
firm involves more loss of control than an HCI could tolerate.

The patterns for the other types of leaders when comparing the acquired
and acquiring organizations are also similar. The preferences for the same
type of leader are opposites for the two merger partners, owing to the
differential amount of challenge and control available to each of the merger
partners in each of the acculturation modes (see Table 5.1). For example,
the PI in the acquiring organization is likely to select separation; the PI in
the acquiring firm, however, will try to avoid separation. The SQG for
both organizations will try to avoid change in order to maintain maximum
control. However, this leads to preferences for different modes (see Figures
6.3 and 6.5). The only pattern that is similar for the leaders in the two
merger partners is that of the PM. This is not surprising, since, as presented
in Chapter 5, integration provides relative balance in the exchange relationship.

LEADERSHIP DURING MERGERS: CHANGING AND PRESERVING
CULTURE AND MANAGING ANXIETY

Many executives leave, or are forced to leave, their firms after it is
acquired. Existing managers are retained mostly when the acquired units
are allowed to maintain all or part of their identity. New management, on
the other hand, is brought in, in cases of assimilation. Regardless of who
the executives are, a leader's role as a creator and transmitter of culture
is further reinforced in a merger. In addition, one of the major functions
of a leader during a merger is to manage the anxiety caused by the uncertainty and change. As discussed in Chapter 2, contact with a different

Figure 6.5
Preferred Mode of Acculturation for the Leader of the Acquired Firm

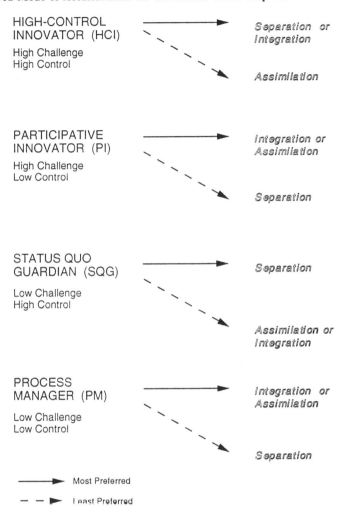

culture invariably creates conflict and tension. The leader has a primary responsibility to ensure some level of employee participation, as their becoming part of the transition process may be one of the most crucial factors in helping to reduce this tension.

Preserving and Changing Culture

Whether an organization will merge with its partner through assimilation, integration, or separation, the leader has the responsibility to make sure that the culture changes according to his or her own preferences and those of the other organization members. So the leader becomes a symbol of culture during the merger. The potential threats to the cultures of both organizations makes preservation of some or all cultural elements central, since their loss would lead to a loss of identity. Given the centrality of the role of the leader in the creation and maintenance of culture (see Chapter 2), the leader has an essential role in helping the organization to maintain all or part of its culture or to relinquish it and adopt another. After a merger, a large percentage of the decisions made by the leader of the acquired firm cease to be made independently and are instead arrived at through negotiation with the executives of the parent company.

Role Model. By virtue of his or her behavior, the leader can send powerful signals about how employees should react to the merger and how they should handle its implementation. Given reasonable trust and good faith, employees should follow their leader's example and treat the merger partner as he or she does. If the leader is combative and resisting the process, employees are likely to follow suit. On the other hand, the leader's cooperation and professionalism during the merger and behind closed doors are likely to be a model for others.

When the culture has to be changed, as is the case in integration, the leader is likely to spearhead the process. He or she can help the organization make sense of the other culture and formally and informally negotiate the changes to the organization's benefit. For example, the leaders of the two organizations are responsible for decisions on the changes in structure. Who will be reporting to whom in the new organization? How will titles be changed? How centralized will decision making be? The behavior and attitude of the leader are likely to be used as a gage by others within the organization to indicate the climate and progress of the merger.

Reward System. The reward system controlled by the leader can be used as a way of encouraging agreement on the preferred mode of acculturation. Individuals who are in agreement with the acculturation decisions are likely to be rewarded in a variety of ways, whereas those who are not will eventually be pushed out. If the leader uses the reward system fairly and in accordance with the agreements reached within the organization regarding acculturation, it is likely to be highly effective. However, if the system is used to impose the leader's own choice, resistance is likely to occur.

Hiring. The hiring and promotion of individuals who support the selected strategies for the merger go hand in hand with the use of the reward system. The leader's role in supporting the organization to manage change is to select individuals who will maneuver change judiciously and who are skillful in reducing employees' anxieties. Overall, the selection process can be used by the leader as a means of introducing a new culture or preserving the old one. For example, if separation is the selected mode, then the hiring patterns should not be drastically different from those prior to the merger. On the other hand, in assimilation the leader of the acquired organization is likely to lose much of his or her hiring power, whereas the leader of the acquiring firm is likely to appoint his or her managers to the new unit, a crucial step in changing the acquired firm to fit with the parent company.

Structure and Strategy. The independent structure and strategy of an organization are often one of the major indicators of its identity. Depending on the mode of acculturation, they may change. For instance, in assimilation and integration, structural and strategic changes are made in conjunction with the merger partner. The leader's role, however, still remains important. Decisions regarding structure and strategy should be aimed at reinforcing the selected acculturation mode. For example, in integration, reporting relationships are likely to go across organizational lines, and the leader's negotiations regarding these issues are critical.

Physical Setting. As a subtle but very powerful background factor, the physical elements that accompany a merger can play a key role. For example, in assimilation, as a result of either conscious decision or insensitive oversight, the subordinate role of the acquired firm is often expressed in terms of less luxurious settings, offices on lower floors, and the like. In integration, on the other hand, the physical symbols should reflect equality. The leader's role once more is to negotiate these elements to ensure a match with selected modes.

Overall, the various mechanisms available to the leader to change and preserve the culture of an organization have to be used judiciously during a merger to reinforce and support the goals of the merger and the acculturation process used to implement it.

Employee Involvement in the Selection of Acculturation Modes

During merger negotiations, as executives of both firms are discussing the ways in which their organization will be merged, it is essential for them to have a sense of the preferences of their employees and managers.

In the Acquired Firm. The leaders of the acquired firm need to determine whether their organization's culture is strong or weak. Do their employees want to preserve it? Are there strong common assumptions even if there are different values and behaviors? Are these assumptions well ordered? Are they commonly held? The answer to these questions will allow leaders of the target firm to determine the strength of their culture. A strong culture will not be amenable to assimilation, whereas a weaker one might be.

A second factor to be assessed within the acquired firm is how the acquirer is perceived. Is there attraction to its culture and practices? Is it considered a valuable and worthwhile firm? Has it been successful? Does it have a reputation for being employee oriented? These elements will indicate the attractiveness of the acquirer. If the acquirer is perceived as attractive, employees of the acquired firm will be more willing to integrate or assimilate; otherwise, they will want to remain separate.

For the Acquirer. Because members of the acquiring organization undergo less change than those of the other merger partner, their involvement may appear less important. If the culture of the firm requires participation in the strategic planning process, its members will be aware of the goal for the merger and will help decide on its implementation. If, however, they are not directly involved in strategic decisions, a situation that is very common, it is critical to inform them of the reason for the acquisition and the level of involvement they will have. If the two firms will assimilate, the employees of the acquirer have to be ready to accept and acculturate the newcomers, whereas if they are to integrate, they have to prepare for the change and discuss obstacles and benefits. If the new acquisition is to remain separate, the employees of the parent firm have to respect the autonomy of the other unit. In all cases, consultation by the leader will lead to uniform implementation of the merger.

Getting Information. Information regarding the preferred modes of acculturation can be assessed relatively simply in a small firm where the leader is close to employees and has regular contacts with them. More formal mechanisms have to be used in larger organizations. Discussion groups or surveys can be used to obtain answers to the two major acquisition questions that determine the mode of acculturation: How attractive is one's own culture? How attractive is the other firm's culture? Although these mechanisms may appear cumbersome at a time of crisis, they have considerable long-term benefits. First, they force both organizations to do a cultural audit, which allows them to gage their culture and determine their strengths and weaknesses. Second, the information allows for venting of concerns regarding the merger and provides an opportunity to placate anxieties. Third, the participation of employees in the decision creates greater commitment to the implementation of the selected mode. When there is agreement on the mode of acculturation for the merger, commitment is highly advantageous because it leads members of both firms to work on resolving the conflict.

It is primarily the top executives' leadership style that will allow for and encourage discussion regarding acculturation. If they do not advocate such actions, timely adaptation is unlikely to take place. Unfortunately, a common leadership error is to assume that employee preference automatically matches the leader's. Given the size and diversity of many of our firms, such an assumption is a fallacy that can lead to dire consequences.

Obstacles to Employee Involvement

Most organizations, particularly larger firms, do not have a uniform culture. It is quite conceivable that one group of employees would want to preserve their culture and remain separate from the merger partner, whereas another group would be willing to integrate or even assimilate with the parent company. The same situation can occur in the acquiring organization: Some of its employees may want to impose their own culture and management style on the new acquisition, even against the strategy delineated by top management. It thus becomes essential for the leader to, at the very least, inform employees and managers of the modes selected. However, there is a need to go beyond disseminating simple information and to consult employees prior to a decision in order to get a sense of majority preferences. If no common preference emerges, efforts have to be made to reach a compromise before the merger is implemented. Several factors, however, prevent such discussions.

First, most mergers are kept secret until they are legally consummated. Employees hear plenty of rumors and act on them; but there is rarely any official involvement. Negotiations regarding the merger are conducted by the leaders of the two organizations. It is interesting to note that the only time employees of the target firm have any knowledge of a company merger is in the case of hostile takeovers. During hostile takeover attempts, they often become active participants in the fight over the company's ownership. An example of employee involvement is Carl Ichan's takeover of TWA. Although TWA executives opposed the takeover, its employees did not. These employees felt that Ichan could turn around their fast-deteriorating airline. Instead of supporting their management, they sided with Ichan and facilitated his takeover of the company.

A second factor that may prevent consultation with employees regarding their preferred mode of acculturation is the style of the leader. Leaders with a high need for control are much less likely to pay attention to process and to involve their employees. They are also likely to incorrectly assume that there is agreement within the organization, since conformity is what they value. Furthermore, the centralized structure that such leaders are likely to create and encourage will prevent open disagreement with official decisions. All these factors reinforce the leader's unilateral decision regarding the merger.

A third factor that prevents discussion is the assumption that there is really no need for employee involvement, since (1) they are never going to agree and (2) they will "come around" once things settle down. Both of these assumptions seriously underestimate the power and will of employees. Ignoring employees' concerns will not resolve them; instead, it will only add to their anxiety and resentment. Without employee support and agreement, the merger will face serious resistance, and without participation, resistance will most likely be resolved by employee turnover in the acquired firm. Turnover can only defeat the purpose of the merger since the firm was acquired partly because of its resources—human or otherwise—and without them, it is bound to lose value.

SUMMARY

As a major determinant of organizational elements, leaders play a critical role in mergers. Generally, leaders tend to have more influence in their organizations when there is uncertainty stemming either from the external environment or from a challenged or weak culture inside. The higher the uncertainty, the more the leader has impact. In this light, mergers provide a particular challenge for executives, as employees and managers will come to depend on them more.

The leader's strategic type, as determined by need for control and degree of challenge seeking, will have particular relevance in strategic decisions such as merger. The risk-seeking dimension will determine the degree of risk in strategic decisions, whereas need for control will influence the implementation of the merger through internal structures and processes in the organization. These two dimensions will influence the preferences of the leaders of the merger partners in often opposite ways.

The role of leadership in mergers is to preserve and/or change culture. The organization's leaders achieve this by being role models, controlling the reward system, monitoring the selection and hiring processes, making decisions regarding structure and strategy, and implementing changes in the physical setting.

NOTES

1. For thorough reviews of the role of leadership, see D. C. Hambrick & P. A. Mason, Upper echelon: The organization as a reflection of its top management, *Academy of Management Review*, 9 (1984), pp. 193–206; and A. Nahavandi & A. R. Malekzadeh, Leader style in strategy and organizational performance: An integrative framework, *Journal of Management Studies*, (1993), 30, pp. 405–425.

2. See A. K. Gupta, Contingency perspectives on strategic leadership: Current knowledge and future research directions, in D. C. Hambrick (Ed.), *The executive effect: Concepts and methods for studying top managers*, pp. 141–178 (Greenwich, CT: JAI Press, 1988); R. H. Hall, *Organizations, structures, and processes*, 2nd ed. (Englewood Cliffs, NJ: Prentice-Hall, 1977); and D. Miller, The genesis of configuration, *Academy of Management Review*, 12 (1987), pp. 686–701.

3. For research about leadership substitutes, see C. C. Manz & H. P. Sims, Leading workers to lead themselves: The external leadership of self-managing work teams, *Administrative Science Quarterly*, March 1987, pp. 106–129; and S. Kerr & J. M. Jermier, Substitutes for leadership: Their meaning and measurement, *Organizational Behavior and Human Performance*, 22 (1978), pp. 395–403.

4. For research on the age of CEOs, see J. A. Alluto & L. G. Hrebiniak, *Research on commitment to employing organization: Preliminary findings on a study of managers graduation from engineering and MBA programs* (Paper presented at the National Academy of Management, New Orleans, 1975). For research about insider versus outsider CEO, see J. Kotin & M. Sharaf, Management succession and administrative style, *Psychiatry*, 30 (1976), pp. 237–248; and J. Pfeffer, Or-

ganizational demography, in L. L. Cummings & B. W. Staw (Eds.), *Research in organizational behavior*, pp. 299–357 (Greenwich, CT: JAI Press, 1983).

5. See J. H. Song, Diversification strategies and the experience of top executives of large firms, *Strategic Management Journal*, 3 (1982), pp. 377–380.

6. For research about managers' Locus of Control, see C. R. Anderson, D. Hellriegel, & J. W. Slocum, Managerial response to environmentally induced stress, *Academy of Management Journal*, 20, no. 2 (1977), pp. 260–272, and D. Miller, M.F.R. Kets De Vries, & J. M. Toulouse, Top executive locus of control and its relationship to strategy-making, structure, and environment, *Academy of Management Journal*, 25, no. 2 (1982), pp. 237–253.

7. See R. P. Rumelt, *Strategy, structure, and economic performance* (Boston, MA: Harvard Business School, 1974).

Part III

Four Composite Case Studies

Managing Assimilation

As with the other cases in the following chapters, the merger described below is a composite of the many cases with which we are familiar. A variety of concepts from previous chapters have been included to provide a practical working example. This chapter will present a merger between two airlines and discuss the successful implementation of the merger through assimilation.

THE MERGER BETWEEN TWO AIRLINES

When International Air Corporation (IAC) announced its plans to merge with Global Airlines (Global) in 1988, the entire airline industry worldwide was shocked. The merger between the two U.S. airlines would create a formidable competitor that would dominate the entire European, Asian, and North American commercial markets. While the IAC was a strong competitor in the European and Asian markets, Global had risen to the number four position in the North American market. Since there were no major overlaps among the routes of the two, most analysts believed that the Federal Aviation Administration (FAA) would not object to the deal. The firms' executives believed that since both firms were facing stiff competition from many government-subsidized airlines around the world, as well as from many U.S. firms, pooling the resources of both would strengthen their position globally.

Inside the Two Firms

The IAC had achieved impressive growth in its routes primarily through internal growth, and this was the first time it would be attempting a merger.

The philosophy of its founder and current CEO, John Michael, had been to grow through expansion of current services and routes, by funding the venture from internal funds. So the IAC had steered away from rapid route expansion and instead had concentrated on beating its competition on its existing routes. In fact, just last year the firm had successfully warded off a takeover attempt by a corporate raider. During this incident, the managers and employees had cooperated admirably to maintain their independence. As a result, the employees and managers seemed to trust each other, and there was a culture of cooperation that guided their daily interaction.

Global Airlines, on the other hand, had grown to its present position primarily through acquisition of smaller airlines. Its CEO, David Fulmer, had a reputation for being impatient with the status quo and had been able to purchase at least one airline a year since he joined the firm some six years ago. Most of the current employees of Global were those who had decided to stay after their firms merged with Global. Within six months of each merger, there seemed to be a pattern of about 50 percent of the employees either being laid off or leaving voluntarily. Interestingly, those who remained still talked nostalgically about how pleasant work used to be in their own firm, even though in many cases their firms had been losing money.

Competition in the Airline Industry

International Air Corporation. Many government-owned or government-subsidized airlines were directly competing with IAC for customers in the Asian market. In addition, in each market, prices were set either by the government or by some international governing body. Some countries even provided discounts of up to 40 percent over regular prices to their government employees and their relatives. Not being able to compete on price, IAC's strategy was instead to provide a host of extra services for travelers. As such, the firm had developed a reputation for quality in most areas of its operations. In the European market, the competition was even more intense than the Asian market. In each western European country, a number of private airlines as well as at least one government-subsidized firm competed in the same routes as IAC's. However, many of these firms were discount airlines providing bare-bones services. Once again, IAC's strategy was to impress travelers with an extensive list of extra services to obtain their loyalty, and not to compete on price.

Global. In the North American market, Global was known as the premier discount airline. Everything the airline did was based on the philosophy of cutting the traveler's cost. Its advertising constantly reminded the public that Global would match any other airline's discount fares immediately. Its humorous ads even made fun of the other airlines' multiple services and called them unnecessary. The low-price strategy had proven relatively successful until recently. Suddenly, in the past eighteen months, the large, full-fare airlines had started to drastically discount many of their seats and were aggressively marketing them. Having the advantage of filling some of their seats with higher-paying customers, the larger airlines were able to subsidize their cheaper seats. They seemed to be sending a signal to discount airlines, like Global, that they were willing to defend their turf with all their resources.

The Merger Impetus

David Fulmer of Global first approached John Michael of IAC with the merger proposal. Stressing the fact that each airline covered a different territory, and that there were only minor overlaps between their routes, Fulmer proposed that they fully combine the two firms' operations. His idea was that both airlines could benefit from the merger by the numerous cost savings achieved through one corporate staff, one reservations system, one service crew in each central hub, and so on. In addition, IAC could scale back its domestic U.S. operation and let Global act as a feeder airline to its international flights. Initially, John Michael was not enthusiastic about the proposal. First, his organization had no prior experience in mergers, and everything he had heard about mergers was negative. Second, he did not think that the cultures of the two firms were compatible. In fact, he argued with his management team that it would be very difficult to create a balance between the operations of a discount airline and a full-service one.

Having negotiated many mergers, David Fulmer was able to answer each objection with a set of figures and facts. His management team presented such impressive projections of the future of the combined airlines that they were able to convince IAC's managers to give the proposal serious consideration.

After about two months of serious negotiations, John Michael became convinced that the merger, implemented properly, could be beneficial to both parties. During the negotiations, he became aware that Global was in dire need of cash. It seemed that with each round of mergers Global had incurred certain costs associated with absorbing the employees and the assets of a merged airline. In addition, it became obvious that Global employees were severely demoralized as a result of all the cost cuttings and layoffs. Many top-quality managers and employees had left the firm for better-paying jobs in the industry. Those who remained were both underpaid and overworked; yet the firm had a loyal customer base, and its reputation as a discount airline led many travelers to call it first to purchase the lowest fair ticket.

John Michael sensed that with some effort and skill his management

team might be able to save Global from virtual bankruptcy and even preserve its number-four position in the North American market. IAC's cash
reserves would be more than adequate to turn Global around. Since the
deal would be based primarily on swapping ten shares of Global with one
of IAC, no cash outlays would be necessary for the transaction.

If IAC succeeded in saving Global, Michael thought, then IAC could
benefit in numerous areas. First, in one of its prior mergers, Global had
been able to purchase a state-of-the-art reservation system that was the
envy of the industry. Selling IAC's system or merging the two reservation
systems would certainly lead to major cost savings for IAC. Furthermore,
the new firm's customers would be able to receive information for any
flight throughout the world, with IAC-Global flights displayed prominently.
This latter fact had allowed a few key airlines to achieve a major strategic
advantage. Being able to match that advantage alone was worth a great
deal to IAC. Perhaps most important, John Michael was aware that having
a domestic feeder-airline supporting IAC's international routes would be
an invaluable asset.

David Fulmer, on the other hand, knew that he and his management
team had reached a crucial point in the life of their airline. In spite of the
fact that their firm was strapped for cash and that lenders were reluctant
to provide Global with additional credit, Fulmer's instincts told him that
he could still save the airline from bankruptcy. He also hoped that if the
merger with IAC took place, he and his team of managers could be retained. Throughout the negotiations, he was always optimistic about the
future of the merged firms. He reiterated that Global had an excellent
product and a loyal group of customers who would stay with the firm even
after a merger, as long as the low-cost strategy of the firm remained.

International Air Corporation's Culture

Founded in 1978 by John Michael, IAC had a reputation for running an
expensive but high-quality operation. Every individual, from the corporate
staff to the baggage-handling employees, was trained in the "IAC Way."
All employees were expected to be well dressed at all times and to provide
whatever service necessary to satisfy a customer. In fact, there were many
legends about how creative certain employees had been in serving the
customers. Michael always espoused, "If we lose one customer, we'll lose
them all"; thus, employees were very keen in solving their customers'
problems.

The training program for new employees at IAC was so comprehensive
that many referred to it as "indoctrination." John Michael always found
time to spend several hours with each group of trainees and talk about the
IAC Way. No one had ever been hired, at any rank, without first graduating
from IAC's training program. In addition, every employee and manager

was required to spend at least one week every eighteen months in some IAC-sponsored development program. Michael was a firm believer in the concept of job enrichment and had instituted a policy that any employee who wanted to be a manager one day had to be cross trained in many areas of the airline business.

Employees were reminded constantly to adhere to the principles of the IAC Way, and managers were rather intolerant of any deviation from the norms of acceptable behavior by employees. Airline analysts believed that IAC had in many ways a very conservative culture that was based on training employees well and expecting them to work hard. Usually, any employee that left IAC could find a job with another airline rather easily. Wearing a finely tailored suit was the standard dress code for most employees and managers, and the airline went to great lengths to project a polished, professional image to the public.

Global's Culture

As an amalgamation of many airlines, Global seemed to have no identifiable culture except for cost cutting. Originally founded in 1972, each group of its employees had different procedures for accomplishing the same task, and numerous cultures seemed to exist within the firm. For example, while purchases for one department were always handled through a central purchasing department, many other units dealt directly with the vendors. Also, while every employee received the same number of vacation days, each office had a different policy on when and how vacations could be taken. Of course, many of the standard operating procedures were left over from the merged airlines, and managers seemed not to have time to consolidate them into one set of procedures for all. In addition, managers' bonuses depended mostly on efficiency, and therefore most had no time for these rather mundane tasks.

There was no dress code for employees and no formal training programs, except for the flight attendants. Once hired, a new employee was "shown the ropes" during the first day of work and then given specific tasks to accomplish. However, since each individual handled numerous tasks, new hires would soon find a task that they liked and would do it until someone told them not to. New hires were always surprised to see a number of different logos and insignia on different employees' lapels or desks. It seemed as though each time an airline merged with Global, its employees kept their insignia, and Global managers, though not encouraging them to do so, did not discourage them either.

In the past few months, it had become obvious to all employees that Global was not going to survive the cutthroat competition from the larger airlines. Some even feared that Global might liquidate its assets and cease to operate. For the past year or so, as the financial situation was worsening, local managers had been pressuring employees to be even more productive. Tempers had flared between managers and employees, and many top performers had left the firm. Overall, a sense of crisis had existed within the organization that tinted the normal day-to-day relationships of all parties.

International Air Corporation's Leadership

A very energetic man, IAC's John Michael kept a tight rein on many decisions. Two of his top executives, Jim Davis and Catherine Johnson, were the only top managers in whom he confided. Although he trusted many of his other executives, he rarely delegated much responsibility to them. Yet even Johnson and Davis complained that Michael never truly shared his strategic plans for the airline with anyone. Although he communicated well, he was not known to be charismatic. Instead of motivating by cheerleading, he often rolled up his sleeves and did the task himself, leading by example.

An interesting story about his management style was often repeated to newcomers. Apparently, during the airline's third year of operations, a group of new hires was told to help the baggage handlers for a few hours to relieve congestion in an airport close to headquarters. Many irate customers were complaining about the delay in receiving their baggage. Not having been hired for such "menial" tasks, the new employees balked. As soon as he heard, Michael and his entire management team went to the airport and for three hours helped the handlers, while the new hires were forced to stand close by and observe. Apparently, the incident put the new employees to shame, while reminding them that everyone, including the CEO, will do anything to help the airline be responsive to the customers.

Global's Leadership

David Fulmer shared many of John Michael's leadership qualities. He was tireless, he exuded confidence in his subordinates, and he was extremely smart. He also differed from Michael in some important characteristics: He delegated as much as possible and was tolerant of diversity among his employees. As long as everyone followed the general theme of "cost cutting," he had no objection to employees wearing jeans and sneakers to work or to managers running their operations any way they thought best for their local clientele. Managers were allowed to approve new projects and make expenditures without his approval as long as they followed Fulmer's rule of thumb: "Does the expenditure make us at least five percent more efficient?" If the answer was affirmative, managers had the authority to proceed with the project. He often sent out memoranda—of course on recycled paper—informing all employees how one unit or another had become more efficient by innovating a new procedure.

Overall, Fulmer had no great interest in running the day-to-day operations of the business and was always looking for a new challenge. Acquiring other airlines kept him interested in the business. Those close to him reported that his negotiating techniques were superlative, and he was often able to convince the other side that the deal was a win-win situation for both parties. Once the merger was consummated, however, he would leave the details of implementation to his subordinates and start searching for his next acquisition target.

International Air Corporation's Structure

Through the years, IAC's headquarters (HQ) had become the focal point of all decision making. The top executives all resided at HQ and were mainly in touch with other managers within the HQ. Any decisions for which no policy existed had to be cleared by the HQ. In addition, all new policies originated at HQ, and either Michael or Johnson and Davis had to approve them. Once approved, copies of new policies were sent to all field offices, and supervisors were expected to keep their manuals up-to-date and inform their employees of the new policies. Any objections or grievances were then referred to a special HQ management committee, chaired by Davis, with the final say in the matter.

Of course, keeping track of such a large multinational operation was not an easy task. Thousands of fares throughout Asia and western Europe had to be monitored continuously, and aircraft needed to be dispatched to high-traffic areas. In addition, the government regulations of numerous countries had to be reviewed to ensure market preservation.

Each of these tasks and many others were managed by two layers of managers who were in touch with field operatives in each region. These managers reported to a vice president at HQ. Many field personnel had complained recently that the company had become bureaucratic and unresponsive. They claimed that decisions that used to take a few hours to make now took days or weeks. John Michael had charged his executive committee to find ways to streamline the bureaucracy. The committee's report was due just around the time the merger proposal was received.

Global's Structure

Unlike IAC's centralized structure, Global operated with a very decentralized structure. Most of the strategic decisions had been delegated to regional managers, and HQ only intervened if major disputes erupted. Since each region had been the territory of a separate airline before merging with Global, no major changes had been made in the decision-making authority of regional managers following each merger. Except for the unified reservation system, regions were expected to be self-sufficient and not to rely on the HQ or other regions for resources. For instance, regional managers often found it more economical to lease an aircraft on a temporary basis locally than to ask the HQ for reallocation of excess aircraft.

Each regional office had formalized its operations to varying degrees. For example, the Eastern Canada Regional Office had almost no standard operating procedures, and what existed in manuals was outmoded and ignored; yet its managers were able to show that its operations were just as efficient as any other regional office's. The Southwestern U.S. Regional Office was in many respects the opposite of Eastern Canada's. Here, very formal standard operating procedures existed. Every activity was detailed, and no new policies were put into effect without a full cost analysis. Regional managers reported directly to a vice president at HQ. At HQ, as everywhere else, the key strategy was to stay "lean and mean."

Through the years and even after the acquisition of so many airlines, the number of staff at HQ remained the same. Vice presidents made sure that each region's key operations were run smoothly and efficiently. It was not unusual to find the name of the same vice president three different places on the organizational chart. Fulmer was rather proud of the fact that everyone in his staff handled multiple duties and thus earned his or her salary.

All employees were required to purchase Global shares with part of their salary. His philosophy was that as "part owners" employees would care more about the organization and therefore would not waste the shareholders' money.

The Merger and the Months After

After two more months of detailed negotiations, the two parties agreed to merge their two airlines fully. Global became an integral part of IAC and ceased to exist as a separate entity. John Michael retained his position as IAC's CEO. David Fulmer, as the new vice president for acquisitions, agreed to report to him directly.

Initially, Global's employees were very happy about the deal. In the letters sent to all Global employees, Fulmer stated that IAC had agreed to retain all of them and that there would be no layoffs. He further noted that as IAC employees their pay would be increased to a higher scale and that their benefits package would improve substantially. Global employees were very much aware of IAC's impeccable reputation for quality service and knew that it treated its employees very well. Although some employees were reluctant to lose their local autonomy, most wholeheartedly supported the merger.

Most Global employees received the merger news with a sense of relief—especially when they heard that the partner would be IAC. Reputed as an employee-friendly organization, IAC would provide many career opportunities for Global employees, they believed. In fact, many would be able to transfer to some exotic Asian or European country where IAC operated. But most important, Global employees had heard that IAC's training program was the envy of the industry, and they could benefit from it. The constant flow of memorandums and newsletters from management kept stressing the positive aspects of the merger, and soon most employees were awaiting the merger with a sense of anticipation and excitement.

Meanwhile, IAC's managers and employees were viewing the merger with puzzlement. One often heard: "Why would we buy a failed airline with such disgruntled employees? Aren't there better suitors out there who match us better?" Interestingly, Michael and his top executives were so busy with the merger that they decided to communicate with IAC's employees only after the deal was announced. Their rationale was that most of their own employees would not be affected by the acquisition of Global; therefore, there was no reason to burden them with details of the deal now.

Michael later admitted that even he had not been sure about how his firm would be affected by the merger and had suspected that he was ignoring many important issues for the sake of expediency. After all, Global was about to become insolvent, and time was of the essence.

Thus, most IAC employees greeted the signing of the final agreement with indifference and some with hesitation. The latter group consisted of mostly the North American employees who knew their routes overlapped to some extent with Global's. And as mentioned earlier, IAC's operations in the North American market were only a small portion of the firm's total operations.

As soon as the merger was finalized, IAC's top executives started to visit every Global office and immediately replaced all the top managers of each location with those of IAC. The replaced managers were sent to HQ for retraining and reassignment. All Global employees were given manuals detailing the standard operating procedures they were now required to follow. Each office was required to hold ongoing training workshops for its employees, and everyone was required to spend at least 20 percent of his or her time in the next six months in training.

While the emphasis on cost cutting did not disappear, it was moderated. Now, "customer service" became the overarching focus of every part of the organization. Managers were told that while they were still responsible for the overall efficiency of their unit, providing quality service to customers was to be their supreme concern.

The first month after the merger can best be described as "chaotic." While Global's staff was more than willing to accept the many changes that IAC was requiring in their daily routines, they had not been prepared for the avalanche of memorandums and details that pursued—corporate directives detailing how they should dress in the mornings, how their hair should look, how they should greet their fellow workers as well as their customers, and how numerous other daily activities should be conducted. Former Global employees were overwhelmed. Suddenly, the employees became very unsure of themselves. Having worked and behaved in a certain way for years, now they were asked to work and behave differently. As can be expected, most did behave differently while being observed, yet reverted to their old behavior and methods the moment their managers were not in sight. In a few instances, customers reported that the person servicing them at the airport had put on a yellow cap with the word "Global" embossed on it. Many such acts of defiance were being reported to HQ, and the response from HQ was to authorize managers to fire any employee who was seen to violate corporate standards of dress or behavior. Within the same month, about 10 percent of Global's staff voluntarily left the new firm. These employees often stated: "We rather leave than stay and watch the old firm disappear."

Most employees, however, soon adopted many of the procedures specified by IAC. Even die-hard Global employees admitted that the overall operation of their offices had improved. It was obvious that IAC had started to funnel much needed cash to local offices, and new equipment and materials were being purchased. While one would not characterize the new furnishings as expensive, still they were quite functional and certainly an improvement over the old stuff. HQ had specified that although offices were not to be relocated, they were to be refurbished and to become "customer- and employee-friendly." All equipment, from the fleet of airplanes to the counters at the airports, was painted with the colors of IAC, and all the old stationery was replaced.

As part of their training, many of the newly acquired firm's employees were transferred to IAC's local or international field offices. They were to become familiar with the "IAC Way" and then return to their former location. When they arrived at IAC offices, these employees faced indifference. Being unprepared for their arrival, IAC's employees resented being forced to spend time and effort acculturating the new arrivals. A few IAC employees, especially in the North American offices, were openly hostile toward their new trainees. Once informed of the conflict, HQ announced an incentive program under which any IAC employee that agreed to train a Global employee would receive a substantial bonus and preferential treatment if he or she wished to transfer to another office. Michael stated that although the incentive program was expensive, the overall cost of replacing disgruntled employees was much more. Soon field offices were reporting a more hospitable reception toward the newly acquired employees.

Epilogue

Within a year after the deal was struck, former members of the Global staff were slowly being transformed. Now that they did not have to worry about being laid off, many were feeling rejuvenated. Those trained at HQ or other field offices were being transferred back and brought with them a wealth of information and knowledge about their new employer. Since these "locals" were already trusted by their colleagues, they were able to act as catalysts for change. Many reported that since the operations of Global and IAC were completely assimilated, Global's North American operations were now a vital, integral, and inseparable part of IAC.

These reports were quite accurate. Although productivity had not yet reached its premerger peak and costs had increased, there were signs that the overall operations would become profitable within two years. Most important, IAC's international traffic had increased substantially, since passengers were now able to get a very low fare within North America and then connect to an IAC international flight. The image of IAC as a major player in the airline industry was enhanced.

Although both IAC's suppliers and buyers hesitated initially when the merger was announced, they soon changed their tactics. At first, knowing that IAC had no prior experience with mergers, suppliers and buyers had assessed the risk of joining a discount airline with a full-fare one as very high. However, once the decisive actions taken by IAC to change Global became public, all stakeholders agreed that the merger made strategic sense.

A LOOK AT THE CASE

The IAC-Global merger is an excellent example of assimilation as a mode of acculturation. Two related airlines decided to merge their operations fully, and along the way, one was assimilated into the other. Now let us take a critical look at the merger process and its defining elements of culture, structure, strategy, and leadership, then follow with a discussion of the acculturation process.

Organizational Culture and Structure

The cultures of the two firms differed significantly in some key characteristics. While IAC espoused a unified, cooperative, and trusting culture, Global allowed numerous weak subcultures to exist within its overall cost-cutting culture. Being service oriented, IAC allowed its employees to be creative in solving the customers' problems—but always within the conservative boundaries of its culture. Global, on the other hand, nurtured a cost-cutting culture that limited the creativity of its employees. While Global was profitable, its efficiency-driven culture was tolerated by its employees; however, once competition intensified and managers responded by attempting to make Global even more efficient, the employees became extremely resistant and felt that they had already been stretched to their limits.

IAC had a well-trained group of employees who seemed to take immense pride in the organization. All employees were trained in the "IAC Way," which—although some criticized it as indoctrination—gave a sense of pride, belonging, and shared values to all. No such program existed at Global. Therefore, local subcultures were allowed to thrive, without a unifying, strong, overarching sense of shared values. In effect, each local office had preserved its own culture from the days when it was independent. Global's leadership failed to create a unified culture for its entire operation. After each merger, Global had lost up to 50 percent of the acquired unit's employees to attrition and layoffs, and those who remained were demoralized and stressed. The organization seemed to have reached its limits in how far it could pursue its efficiency-driven culture without alienating its entire staff. In sum, the polished, well-disciplined, and conservative employees of IAC were very different from the poorly dressed, disorganized, and not-so-conservative employees of Global.

Structurally, while there were some similarities between the two firms' operations, they differed significantly on some key dimensions. The task of managing both airlines was very complex, each having many field offices dispersed geographically. While IAC had centralized most of its operations at HQ, Global had preferred a decentralized model. IAC's tasks were formalized and adhered to standard operating procedures, uniformly administered by all field offices. Global had many standard operating procedures left over from each of its acquisitions and variably enforced by each regional office. IAC was rather bureaucratic with many different layers of managers, whereas Global remained "lean and mean." The overall effect of these differences was that the firms' structures were incompatible, and after the merger, one or both of the structures had to be completely revamped.

Strategy and Merger Motive

Global's cost-cutting strategy faced stiff competition from full-fare airlines, and its primary merger motive was to survive. IAC, on the other hand, saw some strategic value in combining the domestic operations of Global with IAC's international lines and thus becoming more competitive worldwide. As a related merger, IAC and Global had in-depth knowledge of each other's strategy and through months of negotiations became very familiar with the strengths and weaknesses of each other.

Referring back to our discussion of characteristics of related mergers in Chapter 3 (see Table 3.1), the bargaining power of IAC did not decrease once its strategy to change Global was put into effect. Although the transfer of human resources was indeed very difficult and led to many leaving the firm, most stayed and were retrained by IAC. The required close interaction between the personnel of IAC and Global led to many conflicts but did not harm the firm in the long run. As discussed in Chapter 3, related mergers may take a long time to show results. In this case, the prediction was that after two years Global's old operation would become profitable, and it did. Of course, IAC did not diversify its risks by merging with a related firm. However, the fact that the acquired firm was a discount airline with a loyal following seemed to broaden IAC's overall market, which made it even more competitive.

Leadership

IAC's leader, John Michael, was an innovative manager who stressed that the firm be responsive to its customers' needs. At the same time, he did not like to delegate to his management team and had centralized decision making. Further, he had instituted tight controls over his organization's culture, yet allowed it to be adaptable to customers. These characteristics fit the description of an HCI leader, discussed in Chapter 6. After the merger, he kept a close watch on the implementation process, which was very much in line with his leadership style.

David Fulmer's leadership style fit the description of the PI. He sought challenge and innovation and delegated many of his responsibilities. He had decentralized decision making within Global and instituted an open and adaptable culture. As long as he did not have to be involved in the day-to-day operations of Global, and he was able to keep acquiring new airlines, David Fulmer's style fit the needs of his firm. After the merger, he did not feel the need to stay in close contact with Global. In addition, being in charge of the acquisitions for IAC also matched his style of leadership.

Acculturation

The two firms' culture, structure, strategy, and leadership made assimilation the most appropriate mode of acculturation for both (see Figure 7.1 for factors leading to assimilation).

Choice of Acculturation for Global. The weak and rather unsuccessful culture of Global, as well as the attractiveness of IAC's strong and successful culture, made assimilation the right choice for Global. Global's managers and employees sensed that their weak culture was failing, and unless they dramatically altered their organization, the company would not survive. Their informal and decentralized structure was not able to respond to the threat of much stronger competitors. In addition, everything they had heard about IAC—from its highly touted training program to its highly polished image and professionalism—made it the ideal candidate for Global. Having had a relatively weak culture that was also not successful made these employees welcome the stronger and more successful culture

Figure 7.1
Factors that Lead to Assimilation

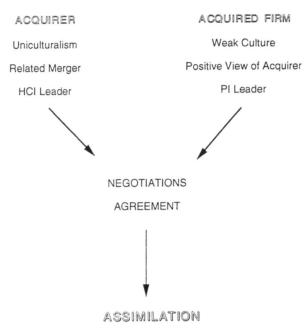

ACQUIRER

Uniculturalism

Related Merger

HCI Leader

ACQUIRED FIRM

Weak Culture

Positive View of Acquirer

PI Leader

NEGOTIATIONS

AGREEMENT

ASSIMILATION

of IAC. For most Global staff, changing their day-to-day routine seemed like a small price to pay for becoming an integral part of a reputable international organization. David Fulmer's PI leadership style fit either assimilation or integration (see Figure 6.5). However, integration was not an option here, since Global was failing and he knew that he could not save it by following the same strategies as before.

Choice of Acculturation for IAC. Although IAC had never before acquired another firm, pursuing a related merger fit its strategy of finding a feeder-airline to enhance its international flights. In addition, being very unicultural, IAC could only tolerate assimilation as a mode of acculturation. Allowing Global to merge with the firm and preserve its weak and unsuccessful culture was unthinkable for IAC managers and employees. Moreover, IAC's centralized structure would not be able to tolerate Global's informal and decentralized structure. As an HCI leader, John Michael's style fit assimilation perfectly, since he was able to maintain control over the organization. Furthermore, his centralized decision-making style fit the need to assimilate the entire operation of the acquired firm. Overall, assimilation was the only mode of acculturation that matched the situation and the leaders' styles.

Keys to Successful Assimilation

Assimilation as a mode of acculturation led to success in the merger between IAC and Global. The key factors for such success were:

- Negotiation and agreement on the merger timetable
- Use of employees as agents of change
- Maintenance of a positive image of the acquirer
- Involvement of employees
- Cooptation of the acquired firm's employees
- Slow change
- Open communication
- Early demonstration of the benefits of the merger

Above all, the intense negotiations initiated by David Fulmer and reaching a mutually agreeable timetable made their final agreement workable. Through these sessions, both parties gained an understanding of other's needs and desires and devised strategies to satisfy them. Second, using Global employees as "change agents" allowed IAC to more quickly assimilate the rest of Global's employees; they trusted their peers and listened to them. Another key to success was the overall positive image that IAC maintained and nurtured. Becoming associated with an employee-oriented organization made it easier for Global employees to abandon their culture and adopt IAC's. Since Global employees were the ones being asked to acculturate, keeping them informed throughout the negotiations and involved in implementation were important contributors to success.

Along the same lines, the merger would not have succeeded had IAC's employees not been coopted to participate through an incentive program. Furthermore, training such a large number of Global employees took time and patience and could not be done overnight. And a final contributor to the success of assimilation was the immediate increase in pay and benefits to Global employees, which helped overcome their initial resistance.

SUMMARY

In this chapter, we provided a case example of successful assimilation between two airlines. Although the strategies of the two firms differed, the fact that Global Airlines was about to declare bankruptcy made it much easier for IAC to acquire it. The two firms' CEOs agreed on the appropriate mode of acculturation. Also, since Global did not have a strong culture, its managers and employees were very willing to adopt the stronger and more successful culture of IAC. Although a few employees resisted the change, most welcomed the opportunity to be associated with a reputable organization that was employee-friendly. Finally, choosing assimilation seemed to fit the leadership styles of both CEOs, which again facilitated implementation.

Unlike many unsuccessful mergers, the executives of both firms showed a long-term commitment to implementing this merger successfully. To that end, all the top managers of the combined firms spent a great deal of their daily efforts managing the postmerger implementation process.

8

Managing Integration

This chapter will present the case of a merger between two computer firms. A discussion of the major aspects of the case will be provided, followed by a number of specific pointers for the successful management of integration as a mode of acculturation during a merger.

THE COMPUTER FIRMS' MERGER

When National Data Systems Corporation (NDC) approached American Computers (AC) in July 1987 for a possible merger, many of its competitors in the computer industry started worrying. Their combined forces would be a frightful competitor. NDC was the nation's number-four computer firm with many international interests. Its primary focus had been on mainframes, of which it was the number-two manufacturer worldwide. AC, on the other hand, had been for many years much more focused on personal computers, and its R&D was the envy of many in the industry. AC had also been purchasing some of its PC components from NDC. In spite of their common focus and technologies, the two firms were in many ways operating in different worlds.

Inside National Data Systems Corporation

Culture and Structure. NDC was headquartered on the East coast. Including its employees in various countries around the globe, NDC had close to 30,000 employees. The operations were managed with much standardization, and many in the firm complained about the bureaucratic red tape and the slowness of the decision-making process. A majority of the decisions were made at HQ and sent down to various locations. There were several exceptions to this, however. Particularly, the foreign operations were given considerable autonomy, and the major R&D facilities were often allowed to "do their own thing." NDC was well known for the quality of its products. Although not generally considered to be at the cutting edge of technology, NDC had developed a strong reputation for quality and service among its customers and competitors. It had focused on cutting costs and had set up its market niche as one of the most reliable computers in the industry. Its employees were instilled with the concept of customer service, and a large component of this service orientation was NDC's extensive training programs.

Up to 7 percent of its revenues were typically used for training, and although that percentage had fluctuated considerably, the commitment to training was still very strong. Much of the training focused on developing sales and contract management skills and on keeping employees technologically current. NDC also provided managers with the latest available management training. Some complained that those programs were too faddish and followed a "flavor-of-the-month" strategy, without much follow-through, but overall, the training had allowed NDC to keep its employees current. Most recently, in response to pressure from customers for increased quality, NDC had started to use teams in the workplace. The implementation of a team concept was far from successful, but the creation of many self-managed teams in a variety of departments had provided employees and managers with an opportunity to participate in different aspects of their work.

Most of the NDC facilities (except for the research facilities) had very traditional office layouts. There were many small offices, with size often directly tied to the status of the occupant. The offices were decorated in subdued elegance with very simple, high-quality, and conservative furniture. There was no flashy artwork. The decor indicated solid wealth with a high-tech flare.

Leadership. Jerry Cole, NDC's CEO, was well known throughout the computer industry for his keen business sense and his uncanny ability to negotiate impossible deals. He had joined NDC in 1985 and had brought with him very broad managerial and financial backgrounds. Both in personality and background, he resembled many of the previous NDC executives. He seemed to thrive under pressure and rarely backed away from a challenging situation, and he appeared to have an infinite capacity for retaining information. Whenever he traveled to NDC plants, he amazed his employees with his detailed knowledge about the operation of the facilities. He demanded the same attention to detail from his subordinates and had very little tolerance for what he considered lack of preparedness.

Some attributed the slow progress of the teams concept at NDC to Cole's lack of interest in the program. Although he had endorsed it, his own style tended to be highly individualistic. He kept many decisions to himself and often used his top management team simply to support his decisions rather than to develop alternatives.

Ever since joining NDC, one of Cole's personal projects had been to find an appropriate merger or joint venture partner for the firm. The pressure from global competition had made him believe that the investment involved in internal growth could be used better by finding an already developed and successful product that would complement NDC's existing product lines. Particularly, the PC market showed the most potential since NDC had not successfully breached it. Several potential partners had been identified in the previous years. However, upon closer analysis they had all been found lacking in one way or another. Some duplicated NDC's product lines too closely; others were in totally different industries; still other potential partners were in weak financial condition or lacked in human resource strength.

Overall, NDC's strong product lines were complemented by a dedicated and loyal work force who appreciated the many development and career opportunities available to them in a large corporation. The firm, however, had mature products along with a bureaucratic and inflexible culture that prevented it from being at the forefront of the innovation that was essential for long-term success and survival. It therefore needed a partner that could provide it with these elements.

Inside American Computers

Culture and Structure. AC was in California's Silicon Valley. It was created in 1980 and had quickly expanded to the national market with a new line of PCs rated by industry analysts as both one of the most innovative and one of the most reliable PCs on the market. The majority of AC's 8,000 employees were located in northern California, with a large group in Boston's Route 128 and several manufacturing plants in the Sun Belt. The recent expansion had also led to the creation of several distribution centers around the country, and an overseas site was planned to join the Canadian operation.

The facilities were spartan. Some of them were transformed hangers. The few people who had enclosed individual offices generally needed them for meetings with outsiders. Like the rest of the company, these offices were designed functionally; they were, however, supermodern and provided a futuristic impression. The many engineers had practical, personal workstations located in large, open rooms, allowing them to interact with each other. There were very few conference rooms, as the open office allowed people to cluster quickly in front of one of the many available boards and set up a spontaneous meeting.

AC's relatively small size had allowed it to maintain a relaxed and highly entrepreneurial atmosphere. It was a "lean and mean" operation. Individual creativity and contribution were greatly valued, and there was a great deal of competition and good-natured one-upmanship among the employees. AC was very much an "engineering" organization, employing a large number of very young engineers who were attracted by the potential for innovation and autonomy. AC operated in a very informal way; the only existing standard operating procedures were found in the manufacturing branch. Because AC employees had a lot of autonomy, many of them formally and informally transferred back and forth from different parts of the organization.

There was very little formal training; instead, various job rotations and an informal mentoring system kept employees up to date. Older employees often talked about their duty to introduce the newcomers to the culture and procedures of their company, and they took great pride in helping the "rookies" along. However, many new employees complained about feeling overwhelmed by what felt like fraternity initiation rites. In recent years, a number of old and new employees had also come to gripe about the lack of formal training, as they worried about falling behind the new technological developments. Many of them also felt unprepared to deal with the nontechnical aspects of their jobs as they were pushed into management positions.

Leadership. AC's CEO, Robert Calahan, equaled NDC's Jerry Cole in his intelligence and reputation for business acumen. An engineer by training, Calahan had worked in some of the best R&D labs in the country before joining AC some five years ago. He was closely involved with the various aspects of his corporation, and being AC's founder's handpicked successor further reinforced his sense of ownership of his firm. He constantly wandered around AC's main operation and joined in the various discussion and planning sessions. He wanted to be kept fully appraised of all the ongoing projects, and he often went to the R&D labs to test a new device or run an experiment.

Although many respected his skill and knowledge and welcomed his input into various projects, others felt that he maintained too much control over too many aspects of the firm. He had kept the right of final approval for all new projects and reviewed most of the progress reports personally. Since he had limited time, projects were not reviewed quickly. Calahan also met with all the new engineers and often invited them over to his house for Sunday brunches. He was the symbol of AC's creative and innovative spirit, and he took great pains to impart that spirit to newcomers.

In spite of his pride in the company, Calahan knew that AC needed to change many of its practices to become more efficient and compete with its foreign competitors. The expensive, and highly successful, long-term, focused R&D operations needed to be supported by other more immediately profitable products. The firm lacked the proper distribution channels to market the successful new PC. The growing number of employees needed more structure and more training to manage more effectively and efficiently.

However, AC had been very careful not to rush into a disastrous partnership. It had turned away several suitors and had managed to keep itself independent during the merger mania of the early 1980s.

Premerger Negotiations

In April 1987, Cole's team proposed to him a merger partner that finally appealed to him. AC was financially sound, with an excellent product line that would complement NDC very well without duplication. The products, although not fully compatible, could operate together. One of AC's most valuable assets was its young, promising work force. AC had attracted a group of highly specialized, creative young engineers, and its management had been able to preserve and encourage that creativity. In addition, Cole respected and liked Calahan, whom he had met on several previous occasions.

Calahan, for his part, heard about NDC's research into his firm and started his own investigation into NDC. Although being part of a large bureaucracy did not appeal to him, much of what NDC had to offer was attractive. Calahan was confident that he could keep NDC out of his day-to-day operations, thereby "having his cake and eating it, too."

When in June 1987 Cole and his management team approached Calahan to propose a merger, they found him to be interested. Calahan very quickly had several meetings with his top managers and, in a highly unusual move, decided to discuss the proposal with AC's employees. Their response was a guarded positive one. As with Calahan himself, their major concern was the preservation of their independence. They wanted to continue doing things "their way." The more bureaucratic, less flexible NDC culture did not fit well with their "lean and mean" practices. On the other hand, many managers were excited about the cash influx and the negotiating power that the merger could bring their firm. AC employees were also eager to take advantage of NDC's extensive training and development programs.

In addition to the legal and financial negotiations that were conducted to consummate the merger, much of the discussion centered around AC's concerns about managerial and cultural interference from NDC. As a result, NDC made several promises to allow AC to remain independent. Calahan and his top management team would stay in place, retain their titles and responsibilities, and continue operating AC. Calahan would sit on NDC's board and become part of its Strategic Planning Council. The newly formed firm would be called NDC-AC, and a new logo would replace both NDC's and AC's old ones. The two firms also agreed that their employees would transfer between them easily and established a variety of mechanisms that allowed for AC's employees to take advantage of NDC's training programs. On the other hand, in a move intended to revitalize NDC's R&D, Cole proposed that a number of AC's top engineers and managers join NDC's major research facilities located in northern California.

The negotiations were detailed and lengthy. Calahan continued to involve many of his employees. The tone was highly cooperative and cordial. Several teams of AC employees even visited NDC facilities, and although they poked fun at all the unnecessary luxury and their counterparts' formal business attire, they were generally impressed. Because of the careful planning and extensive preparation that were being done, many business analysts had high hopes for the merger.

The Day After and Beyond

After the merger was legally consummated in December 1987, NDC kept a majority of its promises. The new firm was called NDC-AC. Very few AC top managers were pushed out, although some left voluntarily because of their lack of confidence in NDC's capability to keep AC's unique entrepreneurial qualities. The two firms' markets remained largely separate, but NDC's considerable and highly skilled sales force started selling AC products. AC gained instantaneous access to NDC's global market, and the two firms started sharing many of their distribution channels. In spite of Cole's single-minded leadership, he welcomed Calahan's input into the strategic planning process, and the two quickly and surprisingly developed a friendship.

There were some changes at AC's major facilities, but most did not cause considerable upheaval. Day-to-day operation was not affected. Many AC employees did not even see or talk to an NDC manager or employee. AC managers and employees remained in place. Managers were saddled with new paperwork that allowed for tighter financial control. The review process for funding new projects was formalized and became more cumbersome. Whereas, in spite of Calahan's delays, it often took less than a month to start up a new project, now NDC imposed a lengthier process that could take up to six months. However, once funded, projects benefited from considerably more resources both financial and otherwise. Several project managers at AC were able to purchase equipment and hire employees to work on their projects, whereas prior to the merger, such expenses would be considered impossible. As a result, the bureaucratic process was, by and large, tolerated, since it provided for added resources.

One of the most favorable changes, which led to contact between the two groups, was access to training programs. Although it took over seven months for the first AC employees to participate in NDC training, they were delighted with the programs and brought back much up-to-date knowledge and new ideas. AC managers received training in basic managerial and marketing functions and were introduced to current management thought. Participation in NDC training programs provided AC employees with a glimpse into the best aspect of their parent company and strengthened their relationship.

In spite of the relative smoothness of most of the exchanges between the two firms, there were several highly visible clashes, some examples of which follow.

The Logo Battle. The logo change became a highly debated issue. The first logo proposed resembled NDC's old one too much, and AC executives refused to accept it. The second one had AC's gray and blue colors and prompted NDC executives to ask, "Who purchased whom?" After lack of agreement on the third try, Cole and his management team selected a new logo highly similar to NDC's old one, as it kept the NDC colors and only seemed to change the old logo form slightly.

Having to use what they considered to be NDC's logo in spite of many promises infuriated AC employees, who then continued to use their old letterhead—in spite of repeated requests and threats from various upper management groups—until they ran out. More important, five of AC's top engineers quit their jobs several weeks after this incident to form their own firm, citing the logo decision as a sign of things to come. This turnover served a very strong blow to both firms and threatened to destroy the positive atmosphere that was prevalent prior to its occurrence. Even two years after the merger, many AC employees still had some of the old letterhead stationery and business cards and recalled the logo battle bitterly. This battle, which they felt they had lost, was for them the symbol of their new subservient status in the new company.

Sales Arguments. The sales departments of the two firms were involved in constant arguments in spite of the fact that they were not in competition. Each complained about having to take care of the other and having to do their job for them. AC products were now sold through NDC's sales force and distribution centers. NDC's sales lacked both interest in, and close knowledge of, AC products. They also inherited several of AC's previous customers, who often complained about missing the personal touch they got from AC. When they asked AC people for help, they were often ignored and treated in a very perfunctory manner. When asked about her lack of cooperation, one AC saleswoman said: "They wanted our product. They are supposed to be the big company; let them figure it out. Nobody trained me; I learned on my own. Why can't they do that?" Another said: "I don't understand why they need to know all this stuff. I sometimes think they are going to take over our department. What is going to happen to us then?" As a result, either AC products were not sold consistently or customer accounts did not receive the necessary attention.

On the other hand, many of AC's customers showed interest in NDC products. AC's sales force had no knowledge of them and in many cases did not even bother letting NDC people know about their potential new clients.

The conflict between the two groups caused both of them to lose many accounts and much customer confidence. The problem was finally handled by a series of training seminars. First, the AC sales force was asked to put together a comprehensive training program for the NDC people. Several liaison employees were also identified and assigned as troubleshooters. Second, AC employees participated in several NDC sales training programs. Finally, the two sales departments instituted an exchange program that required managers and salespeople to rotate between the two firms. Although it was both impractical and impossible to totally exchange all the employees, many of the first transfers came back to their initial company more knowledgeable and were able to convey important information, thereby making the program a success.

Battle in the Lab. Based on premerger agreements as part of an exchange program between the two firms, the first eight senior AC engineers transferred to NDC's northern California research facility. Although these eight were wary of NDC's ability to run an R&D lab, they were looking forward to having the opportunity to work with a vast talent pool and secretly relished showing the new parent company what it takes to be good at innovation. For many AC employees, the transfer of these first engineers was the symbol of their being on equal footing with the new parent firm. As one AC employee put it: "We have no use for their people, and nobody from NDC has come to our facilities. They need our help. That makes me feel great."

The AC's engineers' transfer was barely noticed at NDC. The lab director saw them a week after their arrival. It appeared as if they were not expected at all. When they finally met with the director, he told them he was pleased they had come to be "trained" here and assigned them each to a different project. A few of the engineers in the NDC project teams had never heard of the AC merger. Others were ready to "show the new guys how it's done in a real operation." Contrary to their expectations, the AC transfers did not participate in any of the planning meetings or the projects reviews. They were either ignored or treated like the "poor cousins" who have come to visit. Many NDC employees were highly condescending to them and refused to involve them in any substantial research activities. This not only offended the AC engineers, but it also disappointed them, because in spite of their very brief stay at NDC, they already had many ideas on how to restructure various aspects of research activities, and they were eager to have a chance to discuss and implement them.

The news of the situation got back to AC quickly. In spite of his generally positive relationship with Cole, Calahan could not get through to Cole and had to deal with several of his executives, who could not understand why there was such a big fuss. It took Cole's personal intervention with the NDC research facility director several weeks later to clarify the role of AC engineers. His intervention provided the engineers with a more formal role but fueled the resentment that already existed. Calahan, who was furious about the incident, unilaterally recalled his engineers, an action that led to a heated exchange with Cole. As a resolution was not in sight, the transfer project was put on hold indefinitely, thereby depriving NDC of the achievement of one of its merger goals.

Outside View. From the outside, the merger looked like a match made in heaven. The financial planning seemed to have been precise and correct. In spite of clashes, the level of goodwill and cooperation was exemplary in times of hostile takeovers and nasty tender offers. There was very little interference from NDC, and two years after the merger, many AC officers were still in place. Participation of AC employees in NDC training programs became one of the major vehicles for the slow socialization into NDC culture and practices. Many AC employees returned from training and tried to implement the various programs they had learned, thus slowly changing their culture. In particular, the use of teams started to become a standard practice at AC.

Epilogue

Four years after the merger, every AC executive who left the firm was replaced with an NDC person—a sore point for AC employees who do not see many chances for moving up to higher management in their own company. Although the official name of the firm is NDC-AC, the AC part is often left off in official communication. Many refer to the old AC as if it does not exist anymore. A large group of current AC employees was hired after the merger and therefore has no knowledge of the old company. Notwithstanding the changes and NDC's relative domination, AC has maintained much of its culture and is still one of the most autonomous NDC facilities. Its focus has remained research, and the entrepreneurial spirit is still predominant. The organization is very loosely structured and still functions like an academic R&D lab. The influx of cash from NDC has allowed much improvement in the facilities, and the training programs have ensured continued technical expertise.

Although the changes at NDC were less noticeable than those at AC, some aspects of NDC were affected by the merger. AC's PC has become a fully integrated part of NDC's product line. Several of NDC's research facilities are run by old AC engineers. These facilities have been provided with even more autonomy than they enjoyed before the merger, and their position as innovators in the industry has been strengthened. NDC was, and continues to be, a highly political bureaucracy, where most people are very careful about their behavior and activities. However, the contact with the highly open and often painfully direct AC executives and managers has been a rude awakening and has created some change in managerial practices. There is much disagreement and discussion, often fueled by Calahan, who has remained both as AC's president and as a member of NDC's board. The more open atmosphere fits well with the team building efforts; so it has been well accepted, although not always easily implemented.

A LOOK AT THE CASE

The NDC-AC merger exemplifies how two firms can use integration as the primary mode of acculturation during a merger. The two firms combined some of their operations while keeping many of them separate.

Organizational Culture and Structure

The two firms have both a number of similarities and a number of differences. Although they both manufacture computers, they have very different markets and focuses. NDC is primarily a computer manufacturer with several research facilities. AC is a research facility that also manufactures computers. Whereas NDC is bureaucratic and rule bound, AC is entrepreneurial and loosely structured—a difference caused by the age and size of the two firms. NDC is more mature and substantially larger, two factors that often lead to the development of more standardized, less flexible structures and cultures. On the other hand, its size and geographic dispersion had forced NDC to decentralize decision making to some extent and to allow independence to a number of its divisions, demonstrating the tolerance of different cultures within the organization. As compared with NDC, AC is at an earlier stage of development, smaller than its partner, and therefore much less formalized. Its smaller size allows it to be flexible.

Both cultures are very strong. Employees in both firms identify with the culture. In AC, the culture is transferred and reinforced through informal, but highly powerful, individual mentoring and socializing of new employees. NDC perpetuates its culture through its extensive training and development, which instill the current and future culture in employees. Employees of both firms are loyal and dedicated, which signifies satisfaction not only with the organization but also with its culture. Interestingly, although the cultures of the two firms are very different, they are both successful in that they support the organization in accomplishing its goals.

Strategy and Merger Motive

NDC's strategy for the merger was to find a firm whose product would be complementary to its own, so the goal was to find a related but not identical partner. AC was in the same general industry, sharing some of its technology with NDC, but the two firms were in different markets. The merger between the two can be classified as a concentric merger (see Chapter 3). A concentric merger still falls in the related category, although the relatedness of the two firms is not on all levels. The NDC-AC merger presented many of the characteristics of concentric mergers described in Chapter 3. The relatively few attempts at transferring human and other resources only succeeded with much negotiation. The implementation time for the merger was about two years. For example, it took the sales forces of the two firms about two years to succeed in their joint efforts.

AC's motives for the merger were very simple. From the strategic and financial points of view, it needed access to markets and resources. From the human resources point of view, its lack of training and development programs affected its growth potential. Another overwhelming require-ment for AC was the ability to maintain its independence. Like many other young firms, AC had the potential to grow but needed both the managerial and financial expertise of a more mature firm to continue that growth.

Leadership

The leaders of the two merger partners have very similar leadership styles. They are both intelligent and respected by their peers and employ-ees. They both welcome change and innovation and seek challenge, and they also maintain close control over their organizations. So they are both HCIs who seek challenge in the formulation of strategy and maintain close control in its implementation. In Calahan's case, such close control is to some extent appropriate, given AC's small size and informality, but it has also caused slowness in decision making (e.g., for new project approval). It also keeps him highly involved in the running of his company and the preservation of its culture after the merger. In Cole's case, his challenge seeking makes him undertake the search for a merger partner. His need for control keeps him closely involved in the choice of the merger partner and in the negotiations.

Acculturation

The culture of the two firms, NDC's merger motive and strategy, and the leaders' styles all point to integration as the mode of acculturation (see Figure 8.1 for a summary of factors leading to integration).

Choice of Acculturation for AC. The strength of AC's culture and the degree of attraction to NDC determine the choice of acculturation mode. AC's culture is strong, and employees of the firm want to preserve it. At the same time, there is some attraction to NDC. In particular, NDC's training programs and its success and power in its industry cause it to be

Figure 8.1
Factors that Lead to Integration

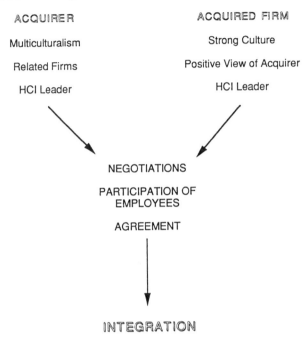

viewed positively by AC employees. These two factors make integration the choice of acculturation for AC employees. In such a mode, they are allowed to preserve their culture while at the same time they can exchange various organizational elements with their new parent company. The main exchanges are in terms of training and development and financial and technological support.

In addition, given Cole's HCI style, it is essential for him to maintain some control over the organization. Separation or integration would be the only appropriate choices for him (see Figure 6.5). The premerger agreements that were honored by NDC allowed him to do so. In addition to his traditional functions, Cole remained as a symbol and guardian of AC practices and culture. His continued involvement assured his employees about the status of their firm with the new parent and allowed them to retain their identity as separate and somewhat equal to NDC. Cole also became the carrier of AC culture into NDC, a factor that permitted cultural exchange between the two firms rather than total domination by NDC.

Choice of Acculturation for NDC. The choice of acculturation for the acquirer hinges on the degree of which it is multicultural and can tolerate differences and diversity within itself and its strategy. As it was for AC, the choice for NDC pointed to integration. NDC is multicultural, allowing some of its divisions autonomy when they needed it to succeed. Their agreement to allow AC executives to remain in place and their interest in learning and using AC practices are further evidence of NDC's multiculturalism. By allowing AC to maintain its culture, they further supported the strategic goal of the merger. The merger was concentric, with the goal of revitalizing some aspects of NDC and complementing its product lines. If AC had been forced to give up all of its practices and a majority of its employees and managers had been forced out, NDC would have failed to take advantage of the strength of its new acquisition.

Jerry Cole's leadership style suggests that he will need some control over the acquisition. Although assimilation may have been his primary preference (see Figure 6.3), integration also satisfies his need for control. Such a need can be positive, as was the case with his involvement in the lab crisis described earlier. It can also take on an authoritarian tone, as was the case with the logo battle.

All the elements in this case point to integration as the most appropriate mode of acculturation for this merger. Quite important, agreement on the mode was reached prior to engaging in the implementation of the merger. Agreement is key to the success of the merger, regardless of the mode selected.

What Was Done Well

Several factors contributed to the relative success of integration in the NDC-AC case. First and most important, based on all the factors described above, it was the appropriate mode for this merger. Whether because of luck, business instinct, good sense, or knowledge of and sensitivity to culture, the various parties in this merger decided to integrate, which meant a relatively balanced exchange that allowed both firms to keep their culture. Another factor that helped the success of the integration process was careful negotiation and planning before the merger. The negotiations specifically dealt with cultural factors and were not rushed. Furthermore, the involvement of AC employees allowed for identification of an acculturation mode that fit their needs and preferences and enhanced their positive impression of NDC.

The role of both leaders was key in that their actions and behaviors set the tone of the merger. The development of their friendship and the respect they had for each other, along with the relatively cordial tone of the negotiations, also indicated that the opportunity for open exchange existed. The exchanges between the two firms were generally limited and carefully planned, though not well developed, and took place only when needed. NDC managers did not invade AC, and only necessary directives were sent—for example, directives concerning the approval of new projects. As a final and highly symbolic factor, the efforts to create a new logo—although they ultimately failed—created a sense of goodwill and cooperation. Keeping both company names also signaled the attempt to keep the two firms on equal footing. These last factors are particularly essential in order for the members of the acquired firm to accept the merger.

Mistakes to Avoid

In spite of their generally successful approach to merger implementation, NDC and AC could have avoided several mistakes. First, the unilateral decision by Cole and his managers in the selection of the logo for the new company was a strong blow to the spirit of integration of the two firms. Although only symbolic, the logo provided a powerful sign of identity. Its loss meant that integration was not a reality and created unnecessary resentment. Furthermore, the implementation of the merger could have been helped by involving NDC employees in the choice of the acculturation mode. Short of involvement, they had to be clearly informed about the planned relation of the two firms to avoid incidents such as those in the lab. Furthermore, although extensive premerger planning and negotiation took place, they were not sustained once the merger was consummated. The careful premerger plans were not implemented, and there was no follow-through. In addition, the various groups that were to be integrated were uninformed and not prepared for this level of contact.

SUMMARY

The NDC-AC merger is one of the few successful ones. The initial care that was taken to address cultural factors is unique; so is NDC's decision to allow AC to maintain the culture that made it an attractive partner. The preservation of that culture was key to the retention of the highly valued AC employees and managers. Too many acquirers destroy the cultural elements that may be essential to their acquisition's success, thereby reducing—and in some cases, destroying—the positive outlook for the merger.

In order to make integration successful, several factors are essential:

- Negotiation and agreement
- Involvement of employees of both firms
- Involvement of leaders
- Slow and carefully planned contact
- Limited contact
- Respect for symbols
- Appropriate/equal use of acquired firm's contributions
- Long-term implementation planning

As is the case with all other modes, negotiation and evaluation of acculturation preferences must begin premerger and continue postmerger with ongoing renegotiation and reevaluation. The employees of both firms have to, at the very least, be informed of the decisions that will affect them most. Their increased involvement allows for more commitment in the implementation process and therefore can be highly beneficial. During integration, given the degree of contact and exchange needed between the employees and managers of the two firms, such contact has to be planned carefully and must be gradual and accompanied by much discussion and negotiation.

Finally, careful attention must be given to symbols. Many managers consider them "silly" and dismiss their power. However, the mindful and prudent regard for cultural symbols reinforces the message of cooperation and equality that is essential in integration.

9

Managing Separation

THE MERGER BETWEEN BIOGENE AND INDUSTRIAL CONTROL MANUFACTURER

At 9:00 P.M. one Sunday evening in 1988, Dr. Judy Thompson, CEO of Biogene, Inc., received a frantic phone call at home from her longtime friend Peter Wood: "We are about to be taken over! Can you help?"

Apparently, a very large manufacturer of industrial automation control systems had just made a hostile bid for Peter Wood's firm, Industrial Control Manufacturer (ICM). As CEO of ICM, Wood was looking at every possible option to ward off the unwanted suitor. But his options were very limited. Not suspecting that his highly profitable firm may become a target for a raider, Wood had not seen the necessity of enacting antitakeover defenses, such as poison pills or even golden parachutes. Thus, the hostile bid had taken his firm by surprise. After desperately seeking expert advice from many consultants, lawyers, and market analysts, he had narrowed his options to one: a white knight. Experts told him that he needed to find a friendly company with deep pockets willing to acquire ICM to save it from the hostile bidders.

Peter Wood knew of only one company that was both profitable and managed by a personal friend: Biogene. After a long discussion, Judy Thompson assured him that she would do her best to help his firm remain in friendly hands. After this phone call, Dr. Thompson telephoned all the members of Biogene's board of directors and set a 6:00 A.M. meeting of the board on Monday.

With Peter Wood and his three top executives present, Dr. Thompson informed the nine-member board that they needed to evaluate ICM's request and respond before the financial markets opened at 9:00 A.M. Since

Biogene had never before acquired another firm, board members were very surprised to even hear that a merger was proposed, especially one with a firm that had nothing to do with biotechnology.

During the meeting, Wood made a short presentation about how profitable and successful ICM had been since its inception in 1955. The company's founder had left Wood with a legacy of hard-working employees, a familylike environment, and a conservative culture, he informed the board. He also mentioned that he hoped to continue to operate ICM as an independent entity after the merger, and he was mainly seeking financial help to defeat the takeover bid.

After much debate and a personal plea from Dr. Thompson, Biogene's board of directors approved the merger proposal. The details of the deal were left to be resolved after the merger. Later that day, ICM's board of directors accepted the higher bid tendered by Biogene, and a month later, both firms' shareholders approved the merger plan. ICM became a separate division of Biogene, and Peter Wood, as president of ICM, began reporting to Biogene's CEO, Dr. Thompson. With the merger having been approved, now the two firms' managers began to negotiate the details of their unification.

Biogene's Successful Past

On June 17, 1980, the United States Supreme Court, by a five to four vote, ruled that patents can be granted for gene-splicing technology. A few weeks later, Biogene applied for its first patent in the biotechnology-engineering field. Founded earlier that year by a group of renowned scientists, Biogene had already made some surprising discoveries in the biotechnology field. Its founder and CEO, Dr. Judy Thompson, and her team of nine scientists had succeeded in producing certain enzymes that they knew would revolutionize the field of chemistry.

Venture capital had poured in, manufacturing technologies had been perfected, patents had been acquired, and within six years, Biogene had become one of the most successful firms in this new industry. By 1988, when the ICM merger was proposed, Biogene had grown to a firm of 1,200 employees.

Managed along matrix or project lines, the organization was extremely flat, and only two layers of managers, all with scientific backgrounds, carried out the complex tasks of managing a high-growth, high-technology company. Numerous teams of scientists, each working on different projects, met and informally discussed their discoveries and techniques every day. The open culture allowed for information to be passed quickly to the entire organization, and managers were encouraged to further foster informal discussions and networks.

No formal rules or regulations pertaining to the daily behavior of the employees existed. Dr. Thompson insisted that all employees be treated equally and given the opportunity to grow as individuals. Teams were not allowed to compete on the same projects, and employees were rewarded for failures as well as for successes. No dress codes existed, and informal discussions frequently continued to late hours of the night. All employees had keys to their building and came and went as they pleased, as long as the work was accomplished.

Industrial Control Manufacturer's Successful Past

As one of the leading firms in the United States in industrial control devices, ICM had gone through many economic downturns in its thirty-three-year history. Its founder and former CEO, Jonathan Davison, had built a successful firm that had grown dramatically in the 1960s. In the 1970s, with the OPEC (Organization of Petroleum Exporting Countries) oil embargo and the resultant inflationary pressures, growth at ICM had slowed, but through cost-cutting measures, profits had soared. Building high-quality products at the lowest possible prices had been the key to the firm's success in a highly competitive environment during those years. When Davison retired in 1979, his handpicked successor was Peter Wood. Having served as the founder's right-hand man for over ten years, Wood continued to follow the same product strategy of high quality at the lowest price.

By operating modern plants and installing some of the latest production equipment in each plant, ICM had remained a strong competitor in the industry. All the firm's products were manufactured according to customer's specific orders, and prices were negotiated individually with each customer. ICM had forged a long-term relationship with most of its customers, and all seemed satisfied with the service they were receiving from the firm. Each customer was assigned a high-ranking manager who was responsible for researching what the various needs of a customer were and ensuring their satisfaction. Although the layers of managers and supervisors had doubled in the late 1980s, customer complaints had not increased. ICM's number of employees had grown to over 5,000 in 1988, when the takeover threat was received.

Biogene's Culture

Operating like a university department or a research laboratory, Biogene's culture reflected the collegial nature of its founders. Office doors were always left open, even at night, and people walked in and out at will. No visible signs of status existed within the firm, and only two titles existed: scientist and manager.

Managers had all had scientific backgrounds and had been promoted

through a special merit system that required a vote of their peers. They
had no special privileges as managers, only more responsibilities. Their
primary job was to facilitate the scientists' work through removing any
barriers that prevented them from accomplishing their tasks. In fact, managers' pay was not increased when promoted. Most important, managers
had no formal powers, such as firing or hiring employees. All these decisions were made by teams of scientists who voted on hiring or firing a
colleague. The system had worked remarkably well, and a sense of equity
and equality existed in the firm that impressed most visitors. Raises were
distributed equally to all, and all employees were eligible for purchasing
stock options at discount prices, and most did. In its few years of existence,
Biogene's stock had made millionaires out of many of the firm's employees.

Such a strong sense of pride and accomplishment existed at Biogene that
it had no trouble attracting the graduates of the most prestigious universities
in the United States. Company recruiters gave prospective employees a
tour of the plants and let them experience the intensive scientific debate
that took place in every corner of the organization. One could argue that
each team of scientists had formed their own subculture within the open,
democratic culture of the overall firm, yet all were encouraged to tolerate
diversity.

Industrial Control Manufacturer's Culture

As a manufacturing organization that had gone through many economic
upheavals, ICM had developed a very strong culture. All employees and
managers worked hard and for long hours. Nobody left the plants when
the bells sounded, and most were at work long before the 8:00 A.M. official
start time. Many workers had been ICM employees for over thirty years,
and turnover was virtually nonexistent. Although their pay was around the
industry's norm, their benefits package was generous, though not extrav-
agant. All employees started at the bottom of the organization and were
promoted slowly through the ranks. Managers were always promoted from
within and put through formal training programs. A "manufacturing" men-
tality existed within the firm that had allowed production and engineering
staff to enjoy special status in the organization. ICM was not known in
the industry as a highly innovative firm; nonetheless, it had a reputation
for excellent engineering and high-quality products.

Most of the policies and procedures followed by employees existed in
manuals. Managers often referred to these manuals first, before consulting
someone in upper management. Most of the tasks were detailed, step by
step, at every employee's workstation, and managers encouraged employees to follow these guidelines.

Apart from the reserved parking close to the plants, managers enjoyed
no special privileges. Year-end bonuses as a percentage of each employee's

base pay had been paid every year since 1955. In some years, employees had enjoyed up to three months' pay in bonuses.

Workers seemed to take pride in their work environment, and everything was clean and spotless. Managers' office furnishings were simple and functional. Formal titles adorned each manager's office door, and all managers were expected to attend all company-sponsored functions. Overall, a strong, family-oriented, conservative culture permeated the organization.

Biogene's Leadership

Dr. Judy Thompson, Biogene's CEO, had spent the first ten years of her professional life in a prestigious university teaching and conducting research. Soon she was recruited by a leading pharmaceutical firm to direct their research laboratories. After being with the firm for seven years and gaining some invaluable experience and developing a strong network of colleagues around the world, she decided to establish her own firm in 1980 and was joined by Drs. James Lewis and Stanley Penna. Together they attracted a substantial amount of venture capital and founded Biogene.

Dr. Thompson had a reputation of being an extremely intelligent, hardworking, and demanding individual. She pursued every problem with relentless energy until it was resolved. She always praised in public and criticized in private. She set very broad goals for the organization and left it to employees to devise strategies to accomplish them. Most scientists and managers felt that she was the intellectual force behind the firm, as well as everyone's coach and adviser. Drs. Lewis and Penna seemed to have the same values as Dr. Thompson, and one never heard them criticize a colleague who may have made a mistake. In fact, they often publicized the courage of those who had taken risks and failed.

Dr. Thompson was a strong believer in the team concept and assigned projects to teams of scientists and expected results. She always emphasized that managers were there to remove obstacles, not to order people around; she did not tolerate any turf battles or power plays by anyone.

No one in the organization had a private office or a private secretary, and depending on what projects people were working on, many employees shared the same work space and secretarial staff. As mentioned earlier, hiring, firing, and promoting employees were accomplished through collegial votes, and a very democratic decision-making environment existed in the workplace. Dr. Thompson was often seen in the labs helping to resolve a scientific issue or giving a tour of the firm to some curious reporters.

When she had first proposed the type of culture and structure she wanted to instill in the new firm, the venture capitalists had warned that such organizational systems worked for small firms but would soon reach their limits. Yet in 1988, when ICM's president called, over 1,200 people were employed by Biogene, and the firm had an enviable success record of patented products and technologies, and profits. Under Dr. Thompson's leadership, Biogene had thrived and become a model showing how a firm can strike a balance between scientists' need for autonomy and shareholders' demand for a higher return on investment.

Industrial Control Manufacturer's Leadership

Peter Wood was a highly respected individual in his industry. After graduating from a reputable engineering school, he started working for ICM as a designer in the manufacturing department. Five years later he was heading the department and had attracted the attention of the founder, Jonathan Davison. Promoted to vice president (VP), he worked closely with the founder for ten years and seemed to have the same work ethic. They also seemed to agree on many other important goals such as service orientation and training of employees.

They both wanted a work environment that was family oriented and took care of all the needs of its employees. When Peter took over the reins of the firm in 1979, he knew many of the employees by name and was well respected throughout the organization. He traveled often to the three manufacturing plants and liked to be seen on the shop floor. Through the years, his reputation as a problem solver had reached legendary proportions: Engineers knew that they could rely on him to find simple solutions to problems they had not been able to solve.

Although most of his time was spent in the manufacturing function, Peter did not neglect the marketing side of the organization. He met frequently with his marketing VPs and wanted to know the details of all their operations. He would start asking his managers questions and would not let up until he was satisfied that all his concerns had been addressed. Although his top managers liked him personally, most complained that his appetite for details was insatiable. He approved most of the firm's programs and projects personally, which sometimes caused delays in responding quickly to a market change. But he emphasized that responding *correctly* was more important than responding quickly. He interviewed all the candidates for top managerial positions and made sure that they shared the same values of hard work, honesty, and long-term company loyalty.

He had asked his managers to prepare contingency plans for any emergencies that ICM might face, and each department had a detailed set of plans to deal with unexpected events. However, he had not suspected that one day ICM might be threatened by a takeover bid. Thus, he blamed himself for being unprepared for the takeover bid when it happened and the likelihood of losing everything he had ever worked to build.

He was shocked to hear that the raider firm intended to revamp ICM and make it an integral part of its own organization, effectively disbanding the firm. He feared for the jobs of his 5,000 employees, many of whom had worked for the firm since its inception in 1955. While neither Davison nor he had ever promised lifetime employment to the workers, they had done their best never to lay off employees. If someone's job was threatened by technology, the company had always provided retraining for the affected worker. Peter was extremely proud of the fact that his employees cared about ICM and trusted its management to do what was best for all of them.

While many of his rival firms had enacted antitakeover defenses and golden parachutes for their managers, Peter had dismissed such tactics. He especially regarded the golden parachute schemes as "self-serving and antilabor." He had said that all employees and managers needed to be compensated in case of a takeover; but he had also dismissed the possibility of ICM's ever being taken over. When he was informed of the takeover attempt, he knew that ICM was not prepared for it. Nonetheless, he vowed to fight it vigorously and preserve the company that was entrusted to him by its founder.

Biogene's Structure

As a matrix organization, the entire structure of Biogene revolved around making each project a success. At the time of the merger, eighteen different projects were engaging the efforts of managers and scientists at Biogene. Each project was the responsibility of a team of scientists and managers with different specialties, drawn from different parts of the organization. It was very common for a scientist to be assigned to four or five projects simultaneously, and the managers would negotiate his or her work schedule. The complexity of each project necessitated that scientists be able to communicate continuously with their peers within the organization. Moreover, through constant communication, Biogene managers assured that no duplication of effort occurred in the firm. Biogene had invested in some state-of-the-art computer technology that allowed the scientists to keep track of all the developments throughout the corporation.

While at the time of the merger eighteen teams were engaged in different projects, the number of projects fluctuated constantly. Team managers and scientists were empowered to disband a team if results were not likely to be achieved or to form subteams to work on related projects.

As primarily an R&D organization, Biogene sold its products and technologies to major pharmaceutical firms and received royalties. Usually, one of these companies approached Biogene with an idea of developing a very specialized product. Biogene's scientists, thus acting as the client's R&D department, would develop the product for the customer. However, Biogene retained the patents to all of its discoveries and received royalties from the customer firms for their use of its products and technologies. Biogene had built a manufacturing line where most of its new products were "test-manufactured," perfected, and then transferred to pharmaceutical companies. The nature of the products dictated that the strictest quality standards be maintained, often in areas where science was far ahead of the legislation requiring such quality-control measures. The top managers of Biogene were adamant that any product leaving their ::%s:be "accident proof."

Overall, everyone tried to maintain a work environment that was informal and collegial. Very few rules of conduct existed, and managers relied on the professionalism of each scientist in maintaining the ethical standards of the firm. Typically, if members were violating some unwritten rule of the organization or the profession, peer groups decided on the sanctions to be imposed on them. Violations were rare, however.

Industrial Control Manufacturer's Structure

Starting as a typically entrepreneurial firm with the founder in charge of most decisions and a few functional specialties, ICM had slowly evolved into three divisions, each with its own separate functions, except in R&D. The latter was centralized, and the three divisions shared its cost and staffing needs. The firm had three product lines, each marketed to a separate group of customers. All three divisions' general managers resided at HQ and reported to vice presidents, who reported to president and CEO Peter Wood. Any decision with a strategic consequence was made at HQ, then transmitted to the division personnel. For example, capital expenditures of over $1 million had to be justified by division managers and approved by HQ. Similarly, any decision that affected more than one division had to be cleared by the other two divisions as well as by HQ.

In particular, personnel decisions relating to compensation and benefits policies were always made at HQ and then disseminated to the divisions. A management committee, chaired by the CEO, reviewed all personnel-related policies and procedures and sent directives to all divisions. As the firm's size increased to 5,000 employees, Peter Wood insisted that uniform rules and regulations be issued to all managers and employees to ensure fair and equitable treatment of all. He frequently wrote to the employees and informed them of his future plans.

THE MERGER AND THE MONTHS AFTER

During the takeover attempt, Peter Wood communicated with the employees weekly and personally assured them that their jobs were safe. His letters mentioned that he remained optimistic that Biogene would be a good partner for ICM and would not change ICM's direction or management. "As far as I am concerned," he wrote the employees, "*nothing* will change after the merger with Biogene." Mainly through these types of messages and the fact that Wood was trusted in his organization, everyone expected that after the merger ICM would be left alone to continue on its successful path. Peter Wood praised Biogene's management in his letters to ICM staff and mentioned that Biogene had a reputation for being a state-of-the-art research institution with no intention of engaging in manufacturing.

Meanwhile, Dr. Thompson was sending essentially the same message to her organization: "ICM is an established and highly reputable manufacturing firm, with loyal managers and employees. Our intention is to rescue them from the takeover and allow them to operate as before."

Many Biogene managers, however, were concerned that their projects would have to be postponed and those funds diverted to finance the ICM transaction. They were also concerned that Biogene would not receive a fair return on its investment in ICM. Citing the competitive nature of ICM's industry, they questioned whether the money could be spent on more profitable industries.

Dr. Thompson and her management team attempted to answer these concerns through meetings and memorandums. Dr. Thompson reassured her managers that ICM was, and would remain, a top performer in its industry and that Biogene would profit from the deal. She also admitted that although there might be many other and perhaps more profitable alternatives for investment, the fact that they were attempting to prevent the virtual certain elimination of thousands of ICM jobs by the raiders far outweighed any other considerations. She told her top managers that she would be in constant communication with Peter Wood and would make sure that Biogene's investment was safe.

The next four weeks after the board's approval of the ICM purchase were chaotic for both organizations. Forging a long-term relationship, virtually overnight, and dealing with an army of lawyers, consultants, and financial experts were exhausting to the managers of both firms. Dr. Thompson and Peter Wood had instructed their negotiating teams to cooperate fully and not to engage in adversarial negotiation techniques. While the sessions went well overall, on three occasions, one or both CEOs had to intervene. Apparently, Biogene's negotiators kept referring to Biogene's "taking over" ICM and "winning the bidding war." These and a few similar remarks infuriated ICM's negotiators. They expected to be treated as "equal partners" and made it clear that they would not tolerate any references to "losing" or being "taken over." After interventions, cooler heads prevailed, and the parties were able to agree on many issues.

The agreement specified that ICM would become a division of Biogene, retaining all its managers and its organizational structure. During the negotiations, it became obvious to managers of both firms that the day-to-day operations of their firms differed so much that any attempts to forge closer relationships would fail. The agreement acknowledged the fact that the purpose of the merger was not to obtain synergy in operations but rather to ward off the unwanted attempt by a raider to take over ICM. Therefore, the two firms would operate as before and not attempt to interfere in each other's business. To ensure noninterference, the agreement proposed that a committee be formed to act as a clearinghouse for any communication between the managers or employees of Biogene and ICM.

Although on the surface everything seemed calm six months after the merger, many problems were brewing inside the combined firm. ICM's managers had heard about the autonomy and open culture of Biogene and were quietly wondering if ICM could benefit from such an approach. They were also surprised about the liberal stock options offered to Biogene's employees and managers and wondered whether ICM could provide the same type of benefits for its own employees. They had also heard rumors that Biogene people came and went as they pleased, dressed as they wished, and did not adhere to any formal rules and regulations. Again, ICM managers pondered whether some of their own division's rules could be relaxed.

Biogene's managers and scientists, on the other hand, did not want to be associated with a "manufacturing" division and basically ignored any news related to ICM's success. Yet bad news was not ignored. During these six months, productivity at ICM had declined by about 20 percent, mainly due to merger-related stress. Biogene managers were very much aware of this decline in productivity and used it to emphasize that their firm should not have purchased ICM. They also complained that since ICM was much larger than Biogene, if it ever experienced major difficulties, Biogene's resources would be stretched to their limits. In addition, Biogene managers were aware of ICM's conservative culture and wondered whether Biogene employees would one day don the trappings of a traditional organization, with dress codes and time clocks. After all, there were many examples of innovative firms in their industry that had become traditional and lost their innovative competitive edge.

Dr. Thompson and Peter Wood made many attempts to stop these rumors. Numerous memorandums and newsletters answering employee speculations candidly were sent to both divisions. Telephone "hot lines" were set up as well, and managers were trained to answer employee concerns honestly but were instructed to press the positive aspects of the merger and the fact that thousands of jobs and careers had been saved. Managers were also to emphasize that the two divisions operated in two completely separate industries and what each firm did adhered to the norms of its own industry, so attempting to duplicate the norms of one division in the other would not be fruitful and would violate the premerger noninterference agreement.

Every manager in each division was sent to a day-long workshop on managing employee postmerger concerns. Later, they conducted workshops in their own departments or for their teams addressing how the merger implementation process would unfold. In addition, managers were asked to keep communication lines open and report any major new rumors or concerns to Peter Wood or Dr. Thompson.

Thompson met frequently with Wood, and they jointly visited the two divisions and answered questions. Both were surprised at the intensity and persistence of negative rumors and predictions of failure. They had predicted that telling employees that the divisions were separate and would not interfere in each other's affairs would be enough. Now they knew better.

There seemed to be hundreds of details that managers of each division had to manage proactively. Employees wanted to know much more about the operations of the other division than managers had expected; they were asking very detailed questions about the day-to-day affairs of the other division and would fill in the blanks themselves if managers claimed ignorance. To make certain that managers had accurate information to share with employees, this time managers were sent to day-long tours of each other's operations. And it helped: By the sixth month of the merger, rumors had subsided, and some semblance of normalcy was returning to the two divisions.

Epilogue

Three years have passed since Biogene became a white knight and rescued ICM from a raider's takeover attempt. During that time, many changes took place in the combined organization, while much remained the same. The top managers of ICM and Biogene remained in their respective positions, and no increase in turnover rate of employees or managers was detected. The ICM division posted record sales and earnings two years after the merger, and Biogene's biotechnology business continued to improve its earnings record and sales.

As the firms' managers met and discussed issues of mutual concern, it became obvious that there were indeed some areas of operations that could benefit from closer cooperation between the two divisions. For example, the payroll reporting systems of ICM had been designed for a large organization, and after some negotiation, both divisions agreed to use it for the entire firm's payroll. Another example was the team management concept that Biogene had perfected. ICM managers showed a willingness to be trained in the team concept so that they could better serve their customers. Subsequently, instead of one high-ranking manager being responsible for each ICM client, a team of managers and employees with different specialties was assigned to each customer, and initial customer response has been very positive.

In spite of these and other areas of cooperation, the two divisions remained separate. They provided extensive training for all their managers on how to deal with the other partner without infringing on the partner's freedom. And the top executives remained faithful to the original agreement and did not attempt to interfere in each other's business. Dr. Thompson met frequently with Peter Wood and was updated on ICM's strategies. They both predicted that in the long run they might find more areas of mutual cooperation between the two divisions, in R&D, for example. But until that day, the divisions would remain autonomous.

Peter Wood had privately acknowledged that he never should have promised his employees: "Nothing will change." Instead, he wished he had said: "Many things will change—but hopefully for the better." He admitted to Judy Thompson that he was going to review many of ICM's policies and eliminate some unnecessary ones.

A LOOK AT THE CASE

The Biogene-ICM merger provides an example of separation as a mode of acculturation. Two completely unrelated companies merged to prevent one of them from being taken over by a hostile raider. Despite having had only a month to negotiate a deal, they were able to find a solution that matched both firms' cultures, structures, and leadership styles. Although the merger was a change in strategy for the acquirer, they managed it successfully.

Organizational Culture and Structure

The cultures of the merger partners could not have been more different. Biogene was multicultural and tolerated and encouraged diversity; ICM was unicultural and encouraged uniformity. The former had an open culture that was collegial, democratic, and equitable, whereas the latter had a closed culture that was hierarchical, bureaucratic, and status based. While both firms had very successful accomplishment records, they approached their tasks very differently. As a research organization, Biogene was compelled to give its highly educated scientists as much autonomy as possible. In previous chapters, we mentioned that the higher the regard an organization has for its members, the more autonomy they are given. The informal work environment and the peer review mechanisms gave a sense of freedom as well as accountability to these scientists. The team concept also ensured that projects used the most suitable talents in the firm and that they were completed on time.

In contrast, ICM's culture and structure nurtured consistency in operations. Managers and employees were trained to be consistent in their approach to tasks. All task details were formalized, and employees were encouraged to follow the standard operating procedures. As an engineering-driven organization, much attention was paid to the quality of products and processes. However, most ICM employees were very loyal to their firm and remained there for many years.

The flat structure at Biogene allowed scientists to communicate efficiently without any intermediaries. Creating a work environment that fostered informal dialogue was a key success factor at Biogene because of the complexity of their work. Scientists depended on each other to solve problems and thus needed immediate access to key people in the organization. Decentralization of decision making was also a key success factor. Project scientists and managers were the experts, and they were delegated the authority to make all the essential decisions related to their projects.

On the other hand, ICM's hierarchical and rather traditional structure assured that the chain of command was preserved and that decisions were made at the top of the organization. Most of the firm's success was dependent on improving the process of making industrial control devices. Therefore, engineers strived to improve the efficiency of the manufacturing process through dividing the tasks into smaller units and making sure that every employee followed the detailed procedures. Promotions from within ensured that all managers and supervisors shared and followed this efficiency value.

Strategy and Merger Motive

While Biogene, in an altruistic attempt to save thousands of jobs, was acting as a white knight trying to preserve ICM's independence, it also wanted to make sure that its investment in ICM was safe. Having had no prior experience in mergers, Biogene was taking immense risks in entering this venture. Since this was a conglomerate partnership, Biogene was not in a position to gain any synergy from it. In addition, not being familiar with ICM's industry, Biogene could not make an accurate estimate of ICM's competitiveness; rather, it had to rely on ICM's past record of accomplishments to assure itself that ICM would continue to be successful.

On the other hand, ICM had nothing to lose and much to gain from the merger. As a target of a raiding firm, it was rumored that its divisions would be dismantled and its employees either laid off or scattered within the raider's firm. The fact that ICM had been profitable in the past was not going to prevent the raider from dismantling it. ICM's executives made it very clear to Biogene's board members that they wanted to remain autonomous after the merger. Their main reason for approaching Biogene had been the long-standing friendship between Peter Wood and Judy Thompson and the fact that they had heard very positive reports about Biogene.

In Chapter 3 we discussed in detail many of the advantages and disadvantages of conglomerate mergers. The Biogene-ICM merger fit the conglomerate category. The firms knew from the beginning that they were in completely unrelated industries, and there was no reason for them to attempt to achieve synergy in their operations. The bargaining power of the combined firm was not affected by the merger, since both firms had been very successful prior to the merger and both had developed excellent relationships with their suppliers. The overall business risk increased after the merger, owing to the increased size of the organization. But since the firms had been profitable before the merger and now seemed serious about their separation, the creditors did not make it harder for the combined firms to receive credit.

Leadership

Leaders played a crucial role in the success of this merger. First, knowing that their firms had very different cultures and structures, they did not attempt to force a mode of acculturation that would not fit them. Second, their commitment to managing the details of the implementation process allowed for early intervention in potentially damaging situations.

Based on our discussion of styles of leaders in Chapter 6, Dr. Thompson can be classified as a PI leader (see Figure 6.1). She delegated many responsibilities to the teams of managers and scientists and was a highly innovative manager. Moreover, she had instilled a culture of openness and trust in her organization and allowed for decentralized decision making.

Peter Wood, on the other hand, can be classified as a SQG (see Figure 6.1). He did not delegate and was not an innovative leader. Furthermore, he had centralized decision making in the firm, with tight controls, and preferred a conservative culture.

Yet the two very different leaders were able to agree on the mode of acculturation that matched their styles (see Figures 6.3 and 6.5). White knight rescues can lead to many unpleasant surprises for the acquired or the acquiring firm. In this case, however, the two leaders were committed to their noninterference pact and did not alter their positions later.

Acculturation

Matching the two organizations' very different cultures, structures, strategies, and leadership styles led to the selection of separation as the most appropriate mode of acculturation (see Figure 9.1 for factors leading to separation).

Choice of Acculturation for ICM. The strong culture of ICM, along with the attractiveness of Biogene's culture, made separation the preferred mode of acculturation for ICM. ICM's managers and employees had no intention of giving up their successful way of operating their company and losing their autonomy. Ironically, their success had sowed the seeds to their

Figure 9.1
Factors that Lead to Separation

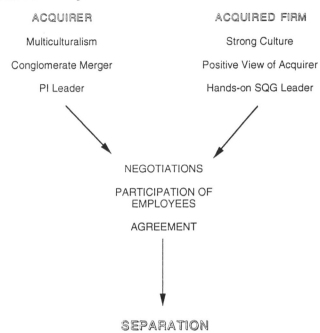

being pursued by a raider. As a company that had an excellent reputation for producing high-quality products, they had attracted the attention of a raider; had they been less successful, they would not have been pursued. The assurances of autonomy that ICM received from Biogene managers throughout the negotiations made the decision to merge that much easier. In many respects, ICM had found an ideal partner for the merger.

Choice of Acculturation for Biogene. As a multicultural organization attempting an unrelated merger, Biogene's executives knew that their organization would be able to tolerate diversity and allow ICM the autonomy it needed. Biogene's lack of prior experience in the merger arena did not prevent its executives from implementing the most appropriate mode of acculturation. Their tolerance for diversity assured that ICM and Biogene would adhere to the noninterference agreement and remain separate both culturally and structurally.

Keys to Successful Separation

During the implementation of the merger, the two leaders' commitment to separation allowed both organizations to preserve their identity and uniqueness. Some of the other key factors that led to the success of separation in this case were:

- Negotiation and agreement
- The leaders' commitment to preserve autonomy
- Noninterference pact
- Focus on the positive aspects of the merger
- Limited contact
- Open communication
- Training of acquired firm's managers in how to deal with separation

Both organizations managed the process of implementation well by stressing the positive aspects of their merger and disseminating as much information as possible throughout the negotiations and thereafter. Visits by the two leaders kept the communication channels open for the employees of both firms. Significantly, training managers to deal with a partner, albeit a separate one, expedited the implementation process.

SUMMARY

Separation as a mode of acculturation was the topic of discussion in this chapter. Using the example of a merger between Biogene and ICM, two successful businesses in very unrelated industries, we showed how the strategy, culture, structure, and leadership of these firms interacted. Biogene had a very open and multicultural organization where very complex tasks were performed through teams of scientists in an informal work environment. ICM had a very conservative culture, with loyal employees, where step-by-step instructions guided employees through a very formal work environment. While the former had a very decentralized decision-making system, the latter's system was highly centralized.

While having very different leadership styles, the CEOs of the two firms were able to cooperate and not only choose the right mode of acculturation but also stay committed to their pact. Their commitment also ensured that the long-term implementation process would stay on course and ultimately succeed.

10

Preventing Deculturation

Each acculturation mode discussed in the previous three chapters has the potential to be a positive experience for all the parties involved. But each mode has to fit the situation, and it has to be managed well. Deculturation, however, does not provide any benefits to the merger partners since it leads to the disintegration of one group. There are of course cases where the acquirer obviously has no desire to prevent disintegration since the goal of such a merger is the liquidation of the target firm. As mentioned earlier, such situations have no long-term effects and are not the focus of this book.

Deculturation can occur even when the acquirer appears to have the best intentions, and it is a state that should and can be avoided. This chapter will present a case of deculturation and discuss (1) ways in which it can be avoided and (2) means by which employees and managers who experience deculturation as a result of a merger can cope with this negative state.

CREDIT SERVICES AND NATIONAL TELEMARKETING'S MERGER

Close to half of this department has called in sick at least one time this week. Almost all of them have been late almost every day! Now you know the rules: After the second warning, CS fires people. We can't tolerate this kind of behavior! Things will have to change and change fast if you people want to keep your jobs!

Nancy Martin was quietly listening to Tom Spinner, her new boss. It was only 8:00 A.M. She had already been at the office for close to two hours, and it promised to be a long day. But this was nothing new. It had been a long three months, and she felt that she was quickly approaching the breaking point.

National Telemarketing

National Telemarketing (NTM) was one of many telemarketing firms that had cropped up in the 1980s. It had started with only thirty employees six years ago and had experienced tremendous growth. It now had close to 1,500 employees and contracted with a variety of organizations to do their telemarketing for them. The growth had strained all the newly developed organizational systems. NTM could not hire people fast enough, and training was a big problem. NTM had started turning customers away and had lost many clients because employees had made serious mistakes on the phone. The company had, however, a large group of experienced salespeople on whom it depended heavily.

Joe Anderson, NTM's past owner and CEO, had started the business in 1981 in Denver and had become a wealthy man. His company had grown beyond his wildest expectations. NTM had prospered, and Anderson used to say that if it had not been for the high training cost, things would have been great.

> We have plenty of business. We have some great telemarketers here. Some of my people can sell anything to anyone. When I started the business, I brought some great salespeople with me. They take pride in their work. They stick around through thick and thin. You have to depend on your people in this business. They talk to customers directly; if they mess up, you lose a sale, and there isn't much you can do about it. The new people we are hiring are not reliable. It's easy to find people; it's very hard to find good people.

Even before NTM was bought out by Credit Services (CS), NTM was going through a crisis. Nancy Martin had been with NTM for just five years. She had two years of college and was just twenty-five years old. She had started with NTM as a phone trainee and was now a supervisor. Nancy was typical of many of the NTM employees. Almost all were young, with little or no college education. They came to NTM and started as phone trainees. Even with the fast promotions, Nancy was not happy about her job. When she had started with the company, there used to be a friendly, supportive atmosphere. Her first boss had spent hours with her, training her and helping her along. Owing to the tremendous growth of the past two to three years, the supportive environment no longer existed and all that was left was pressure for the bottom line. No supervisor had time for one-on-one training.

The trainees received just a half a day of impersonal training, and then they were on their own. The hours were irregular, and there was a lot of conflict as well as a lot of stress. One of the most commonly voiced complaints was the lack of organization. One employee said:

> You can pretty much do what you want. At first it seems great, but it's very stressful. I don't know what to tell people on the phone. I often can't answer their questions. It would be nice to get more information. There are also no procedures for anything. I have been here close to eighteen months, and I have been asking for weeks now how much comp time and vacation time I have so that I can take a few days off. My supervisor says she needs to check with personnel, but nobody there seems to know, so I'm still waiting.

One factor that kept a lot of people was the pay, which was very high; so many, like Nancy, had stayed on. Those who had been there since the beginning talked fondly about the early days. One NTM veteran who had been with the company since it started said:

> We were a big, happy family. Sure, the job was hard, but we all pitched in. We were making so much money and still taking care of each other. I used to sit with new people and just listen to them and talk to them about what they should and should not say on the phone. We worked with people to help them develop their own selling style. It was great. Now it's different. I have no time for that kind of work. There are too many people. They come and go. Who can keep track of them?

Another old-timer, Joe Gargola, echoed this view:

> The CS thing doesn't look good. I've been here almost since we started. Joe Anderson stole me away from a competitor. Things used to be so exciting. We were all involved in everything. Now, I don't really know what is going on. Joe seems to be having trouble letting go. Don't get me wrong. I respect the man; but I think he needs to leave day-to-day operations to professional managers. He is not doing that. He stills wants to make all the decisions. He does not have time for this, and I don't think he always understands what is going on. He is making a lot of people very angry by not letting them do their jobs. The other day, I spent hours with a potential client and had them almost convinced to go with us. I provided them with a whole bunch of information about what we can do. Joe got into the meeting, and he sounded so confused about what we can provide for the client that they left. I don't think they are coming back either.

Terry, who had joined the firm eight months ago, complained:

The job is pretty stressful. You're on the phone all day, staring at a
stupid computer screen. The computer dials numbers automatically
and simply connects people to you. You see their name as you start
talking to them. They often don't want to talk to you, and they are
mean and rude; but you've got to keep your cool. My super comes
on line and checks up on me without any warning. But he never helps
me—he doesn't know much more than I do. Nobody tells me what
to say. The training that I got was useless. The old-timers here tell
me it used to be a nice place to work. Not anymore. We are all in
our cubicles, on the phone. The only time I talk to anyone is on my
break in the coffee room. We try to help each other, but so many of
us are new, we really can't.

Terry's supervisor, Nate Sampson, who had been with NTM about four
years, understood Terry's points, but he felt that there was another side
to the story:

The job is hard and high stress, but we pay very well. Terry, like
many others, has no college education; there is not much else she
can do in this economy. We don't have the best training in the world,
but we do some training at least. Most of our people don't realize
that the half-day training costs us an arm and a leg. It hurts when
our people leave.

Seven years after starting NTM, Joe Anderson was feeling the strain of
running a business. Profits were still high but did not seem to be growing
as fast. NTM had lost several customers. Anderson felt like he did not
know his own company anymore. All the new people were strangers, and
he did not enjoy going to work every day. It seemed to him that his skills
were not needed any longer. He knew how to get customers, but now he
dealt mostly with internal squabbles and turnover, and he was tired.

In May 1988, Joe Anderson sold NTM to CS. He vacated his office
during a weekend and moved to Arizona to retire. When NTM employees
came in Monday morning, they were informed that they now worked for
CS.

Credit Services

CS had in many ways followed the same paths as NTM. The firm was
fifteen years old and had experienced tremendous growth. It had close to
2,000 employees divided almost equally among three centers around the
country, with headquarters in Denver. CS was primarily a collection

agency. It had two groups of businesses: (1) it acquired delinquent accounts from a variety of businesses and collected on them, and (2) it serviced delinquent accounts for other businesses, mainly credit card companies. CS had a reputation for efficiency. Its customers knew that CS could handle their accounts, and it always got results. Because of economic factors and its reputation for reliability, CS was financially sound and was now looking for expansion into other areas.

CS had experienced many of the growing pains that NTM was experiencing. It still continued to have staffing problems, and although the turnover rate had gone down in the past few years, many attributed the decline to the economy and expected turnover to go back up soon. CS had resolved part of its problems by very active recruitment strategies that allowed it to attract a large number of high school graduates. Every new employee went through a rigorous week-long orientation and training program that resembled a military boot camp. The training director, Allen Marshall, described the program:

> We give them the basic sales and legal skills needed to do collections. It can get tricky with people on the phone, and our employees need to know what they can and cannot say and how far they can push. But the major part of the program is designed to scare off the "weaklings." We drill them and give them a taste of what it's like to work here. Close to 30 percent drop out after the first day, and only 40 percent make it to the end. That group that is left is made up of the real hungry, tough folks we need. They can handle anything that we dish out. No fainthearted babies are left in that group. They're great!

CS's CEO, Gary Sanders, stated his management philosophy as follows:

> Businesses baby their employees too much these days. We are here to make money, not to make people feel good. I hate people who come to work looking for a "big happy family." What management needs to do is offer workers good money, show them what to do, and keep them on a tight leash. You can forgive a mistake once, the second time, the guy is out the door. Those who are left quickly learn not to mess up.

CS was very much operated with the CEO's philosophy. The salaries were very good, and fear was the primary performance factor. It was very common to see a supervisor yelling at an employee in the middle of the floor.

Janet, a two-year veteran, commented:

> I am sure that we could all sue them for all the stuff they do. You know, they fire people on the spot, throw their stuff in a bag, and

kick them out the door just for forgetting to use the standard opening line or for not using all the pressure tactics that we are taught. But it's not like you don't know what you are getting yourself into. After that one-week training, if you can call it that, you know what's expected of you. If you can't take it, you can leave. If you stay, they pay well and the work is sort of exciting. You can also move up quickly, which is great. I am going to become a supervisor next year, and I dropped out of college after one year.

Another employee, who worked in the training department, said:

Some of my friends think I'm crazy to work here. When you describe this place, it can sound like a Nazi work camp! But it really is not that bad. You always know what's expected of you. If you forget, they'll tell you. Your job is very well defined. You get good training, and if you perform, you can really do well and move up. But you have to be the type who can handle all the strict rules and discipline. I'm okay with it. I can see how it would be hard for some.

One of the supervisors explained his style as follows:

It doesn't take a genius to do this job. You know you are going to have either a person crying on the line and giving a sob story or a person that gets angry at you and makes all sorts of threats. You just have to know how to handle that sort of stuff. I give my people their quotas and send them off. I check up on their lines regularly; they never know when I'm going to be listening. If they don't do their job right, they get yanked and are reminded in front of all their buddies what they have to do. They don't mess up a second time. They know everybody is replaceable. My boss reminds me that it costs a lot to train a new person, but I have had no trouble getting them, so I don't have to put up with incompetence.

CS had been labeled by a number of employees and managers as an "electronic sweatshop." With all the computers running at once and all the people on the phone, the work environment was noisy and hot. The work was fast-paced, and it never stopped. Many employees worked in fifteen-hour shifts, and there was no shortage of overtime if you were willing to work the long hours. CS offices never closed, a factor that was key to allowing CS to deal with the tremendous business that it was continuing to get. Business was very good, and no one at CS saw any reason for changing any of their practices. Managers and employees seemed to be functioning well, and those who couldn't handle the pace simply left.

Merger Motive. With all the growth and extra cash available, CS was looking to buy another company. Gary Sanders knew that the only way CS could grow fast enough was to simply buy another firm. Very little research was done. Sanders and his five top executives brainstormed, and Sanders's choice was quickly approved. NTM was targeted because many of CS's clients had requested telemarketing. Sanders was hoping that the NTM people would help them grow in that area.

Since NTM was in good financial shape, Gary Sanders personally contacted Joe Anderson and offered to buy his firm. The price was beyond Anderson's wildest dreams. NTM was giving him too much trouble, so he accepted Sanders's offer after his lawyer checked the contracts. The negotiations took less than three days, and CS now owned NTM.

The Day After

Larry Samchuck was the CS executive who was put in charge of NTM. He was a twelve-year CS veteran and was considered to be one of Sanders's closest associates. Samchuck moved into NTM offices with a group of four managers and two support staff. After sending the memo regarding the takeover, they set up shop in Anderson's old office and its two adjacent conference rooms. They poured over company documents and personnel files and requested to see several of NTM's managers and executives. By the second day, three NTM managers, the chief comptroller, and the training and personnel managers had been given four months' severance pay and let go. Two of the five CS managers took over the training and personnel functions; another became NTM's financial manager. NTM's general manager was called in and told to report to a new CS boss, who would be assuming many of his duties. The last CS manager, Tom Spinner, took over operations, and the person he replaced, one of the original NTM employees, handed in his resignation the next morning.

These changes made CS executives feel in full control of the firm. A detailed review of NTM's financial situation further indicated its health; however, there were many areas that needed "cleaning up." Samchuck and his team could not believe the lax discipline: Employees spent a lot of time chatting in the coffee room and around the halls, they were often observed arguing with their supervisors over procedures. In addition, the records for employee work hours and overtime were poorly kept. The CS group was confident that considerable cost cutting would be achieved by tightening the controls.

Spinner was particularly appalled at the lack of clear, written procedures. Each employee seemed to "do his own thing." There was no standard line. The employees' individual approach sometimes worked, sometimes it did not. While some of the more experienced employees were adept on the phone, they did not listen to anyone, and the younger employees seemed to barely make an effort. Spinner very quickly put together several detailed scenarios concerning phone procedures that were to be followed by all employees.

Within the next few days, CS completed its takeover of NTM. Some CS business was routed to NTM. Employees were made aware of their new benefit and retirement packages. The packages were less generous than NTM's, and many NTM long-term employees suffered considerable losses in their retirement plans.

As a result of the changes implemented by Spinner, Nancy Martin and all the other supervisors who now reported to him were faced with a complete set of new procedures for all operations. Everyone was told that they had a week to get up to speed. Additionally, all NTM letterheads and business cards were collected and discarded and replaced with CS material. And finally, the new personnel and training directors put all hiring on hold for two weeks in order to set up a new CS-like program.

After hearing about the new programs, many NTM employees initially became excited. But their excitement soon turned to concern as details of the new programs began trickling back to the firm. One old NTM employee stated:

> It feels like there has been a tornado around here. I was one of those who complained a lot about how impersonal and disorganized things had become at NTM, but now I miss the good old days. It's only been three weeks since we were bought out, but NTM already does not exist.

Another complained:

> If I wanted to go to a military boot camp, I would have done so. The work is pretty stressful without having my boss's boss come down and yell at me. I came here to do telemarketing; now I'm supposed to do collections, too. I feel like the "repo man"! My super seems helpless. That Spinner guy just seems to have taken over, and he barely knows what is going on down here.

Within two months after the takeover, close to 10 percent of NTM supervisors and managers had been fired. Close to 250 of its employees had also been let go. Only a few of the highly experienced telemarketers that Anderson had brought with him had stayed, and those who remained were desperately looking for jobs. One employee reported after having been "told off" by his new manager: "I was just yelled at in front of everybody, and all I did was make a mistake in my monthly report. It was really nothing. I got so upset that I messed up on all of my calls this afternoon. I just was lucky that nobody was listening in today." A new employee who had been hired under the CS training program said: "I am not that unhappy, but the rest of the people look shell-shocked. They talk about an earthquake."

Many of the new procedures were an improvement over the disorganized state of affairs prior to the takeover, providing standardization and clarity. Many other changes were not appropriate. For example, the telemarketers were handed a list of "standard pressure tactics" that were adapted from CS's collections policies. They were too heavy-handed and turned customers off. Other changes were petty and minor but affected morale. The three coffee rooms that were used as gathering places for NTM employees were closed after Samchuck overheard what he considered "CS bashing" being discussed over coffee in one of the rooms. Several coffee machines were installed, but employees were forbidden to "loiter." The break times were shortened to ten instead of fifteen minutes, and this change backfired, as people would literally hide from their supervisors to squeeze an extra few minutes from their break.

All changes—both positive and negative—were simply handed down to NTM employees through memos and posted announcements. For example, Spinner never consulted any of the NTM employees before he put together his scenarios. The change in the benefits package was not even explained to employees; they simply saw a change in their paychecks and, after inquiring to personnel, were informed then. Whenever an NTM employee would complain he or she was told to be thankful for the job and to stop whining.

As a result of the changes and the harsh treatment, on any given day, close to 50 percent of the old NTM employees were late. Many of them took the risk of being caught and made almost no effort on the phones; they barely even followed their prescribed scenarios. One of them said:

I figured out when my super checks up on me, and as soon as she gets off the line, I screw around. I won't help these people make money. I'll be out of here before they catch on. Even if they catch me, all they can do is fire me. That might even be better than working here.

A worry voiced by a number of employees was that they had no idea when the ax was coming down. "The worst part is not knowing. CS seems to be out to get all of us, but it looks like they can't do it all at once, so it's like the Chinese water torture—they are slowly driving us crazy," said a five-year NTM employee. She continued: "I have been going home every night with terrible headaches. All around me people are popping pills like it was candy. Nobody talks to anybody else. We are all at each other's throats. I know I should be just happy to have a job, but is it worth my health?"

Another employee said:

The worst part has been to see people who were my friends either leave or become so involved and stressed out that they barely talk to me. With all the firings, everybody is trying to protect himself. It's become every man for himself. I feel like I don't know anyone anymore. There are a lot of new people. The people in charge are different, and those who were here before are totally preoccupied and have no time or patience for each other. I am kind of lost. This is not the NTM I joined seven years ago. It's all gone now.

Credit Services' Reaction. For their part, the CS managers' early excitement was waning. They were not happy about the progress made at NTM. Their plan was to fully combine NTM's operations with their own within three months, but it looked like this was not going to happen. CS was able to service some of its clients who had requested telemarketing, but the NTM customers were dropping like flies. Only in the past month, three major customers had left NTM, and the profits had gone with them. The training costs at NTM were exorbitant.

CS executives had predicted some turnover, but within three months, close to 30 percent of NTM employees and managers had either been fired or left. As is always the case, those who left were the best people NTM had; the less experienced ones stayed on. CS had trouble finding experienced people to replace those who left, and those who had stayed were often late, used up all their sick days, or left early. They had to be watched all the time. Tom Spinner reported:

I have never seen such a group of lazy and argumentative people. I'm not asking them much. Why is it so important to file things one way versus another? They just don't want to change. As soon as you don't watch them, they stop working. This may sound paranoid and silly, but I think they hide in the restrooms! They are like kids. You have to be on them all the time. When you get on them, then they get even worse. You yell at one of them and the rest get all upset. The supervisors just don't do their job. I have to do it for them. Who has time for this?

A new supervisor, who had transferred from a CS facility, said:

All in all, it's not that there is that much difference between how they did things and how we want them done. But to them it seems like I'm asking them to give up everything. I can see why they would be upset. I spend most of my time dealing with people who are sick and can't come in or people who are so tense and upset they can't work even when they do come in.

About six months after the merger, the NTM facility had become a major drain on CS's resources. Not only had it stopped turning a profit, mainly because of substantial client loss as well as heavy replacement and training costs, but it was also using up CS resources as well. Particularly, many CS managers, supervisors, and employees had to be temporarily assigned to NTM. Few, if any, knew much about telemarketing, and their presence further alienated NTM employees, who refused to help them and often set them up for failure. Gary Sanders now talked about NTM as the "Nightmare on Evans Avenue." Nothing that was done seemed to help. CS even started easing up on the implementation of its policies and practices and tried to encourage the retention of old NTM employees, but that was also met with resistance.

Eighteen months after the merger, CS liquidated NTM. Close to half of the remaining 800 NTM employees found themselves without a job. The rest joined a variety of new firms as the old company was broken up into little pieces and sold off.

Gary Sanders swears that he will never again attempt to buy another company. Rumor has it that he is, however, interested in a small data-processing plant that is highly profitable.

A LOOK AT THE CASE

The takeover of NTM by CS and the total failure of the attempts to combine the two operations constitute a common situation in many mergers. Poor planning and heavy-handed implementation often lead to the destruction of a firm, resulting in the loss of jobs, which is damaging not only to employees and managers but also to their families and communities. The psychological stress and sense of loss that accompany the loss of a job are not unique to mergers and emerge in many other situations.

However, deculturation is unique to mergers in that it is a state in which individuals feel totally alienated from their culture. It involves losing touch with both cultures, remaining an outcast in both. As a result of deculturation, individuals experience a high degree of acculturative stress, that is, stress triggered by the contact between two groups. When the conflict that the contact engenders is resolved positively, acculturative stress is reduced. However, when the conflict is not settled positively, the stress becomes destructive.

Culture and Structure

Although CS and NTM used some of the same technologies and processes in their businesses and had similar growth patterns and the ensuring problems of training and retention of employees, the similarities stopped there.

National Telemarketing. NTM's rapid growth had strained its organizational system and culture. Particularly, the onslaught of new people that were needed to handle their growing customer demands could not be integrated into the business. Newcomers could not be trained properly, as NTM had relied on a one-on-one, individualized training system. And no one socialized them into the culture of the firm; they were left on their own. As a result, NTM's culture lost much of its strength, since it was not passed on to new employees. While they heard about what the company was like, they were not part of that old culture.

Joe Anderson also contributed to the organizational and cultural disintegration that preceded CS's takeover. As is the case with many entrepreneurs, he had trouble letting go of his company and allowing professional managerial systems to be implemented. His style appeared to be that of an SQG. His lack of expertise in daily operations and management was accompanied by a sense of loss of control over his firm. He did not make efforts to correct the situation but simply aggravated the problem by trying to maintain control. His lack of recognition of the needs of a more mature business was partly the cause of the dissatisfaction and sense of confusion among employees and the weakening of the culture and the organization.

As a result, NTM did not appear to have a well-defined culture. Employees and managers were not satisfied with how the organization was being run, and there was resentment over the lack of support from the organization. There was no attraction or sense of belonging to the firm, and many employees remained because of the salary instead of an interest in the business or a sense of loyalty. The lack of loyalty was further reinforced by Anderson's sudden departure from the firm, a factor that signaled the disintegration of existing systems, employee dissatisfaction, and the weak culture in spite of continued financial success. However, even that success was being threatened as clients began to sense a shortage of employee commitment and the lack of unity and clarity within NTM.

Credit Services. CS's highly authority-oriented culture appeared, by many standards, to be too harsh and even inappropriate, but was a highly successful culture. The self-selection process during training eliminated those who could not adapt to CS management style and philosophy. Those who remained were loyal to the firm. The firm rewarded obedience and performance and was very clear about its expectations of its employees. To those who stayed with CS, the culture was attractive. The element of self-selection was, however, essential in the maintenance of its strong culture.

As is the case with NTM, CS lacked a well-developed, long-term strategic plan. Decisions were made by the CEO and his top management team. Control and authority were primary motives, two factors that put Gary Sanders's—as well as some of his other executives', such as Tom Spinner's—management style in the SQG category. They were not looking for challenge and new ways of doing things, rather, their goal was implementation of existing policy and maintenance of control. Partly as a reflection of the style of its top managers, CS was therefore a highly centralized, standardized, and formalized organization with clear rules and regulations and limited flexibility. The culture, leadership style, and structure were all supportive of the goals of the organization, which focused primarily on efficiency.

Strategy and Merger Motive

CS's primary goal in buying NTM was to grow and take advantage of its financial success. NTM's financial success and CS's client interest in telemarketing were the only criteria used for the selection of a merger target. There was very limited planning both in the selection of an appropriate merger partner and in the implementation of the merger.

Although they had very different cultures, CS and NTM were related to some extent. They shared technology both in terms of the equipment they used and in terms of the process involved in the delivery of their service to their clients.

NTM's strategy was not clear, as Joe Anderson's reasons for selling his firm were neither strategic nor related to the business itself. He sold the business for personal reasons. The total lack of involvement of any of NTM's employees and managers in the decision to sell to CS was a central contributor to the events that followed.

Deculturation

The conditions for deculturation (see Figures 5.3 and 5.4) are as follows: (1) The acquirer is generally unicultural and attempting to merge with a firm in an unrelated business, and (2) the acquired firm has a weak culture and low attraction to the acquirer. These factors are assumed to lead to deculturation. The CS-NTM merger presented all but one of the typical factors leading to deculturation (see Figure 10.1 for a summary).

Choice of Acculturation for Credit Services. CS had a very strong, centralized, authority-oriented culture. There was no encouragement of different points of view and no tolerance for diverse cultures and practices. Therefore, CS was a highly unicultural organization. Although CS's geographic dispersion generally should have led to more flexibility, its small size and very strong training program allowed for the maintenance of its homogeneity. In addition, CS's leadership had a high need for control with a low need for challenge (SQG) and it acquired a business in a related industry; so the choice of acculturation for CS was assimilation.

All of CS's decisions, plans, and actions were aimed at combining NTM

Figure 10.1
Factors that Lead to Deculturation

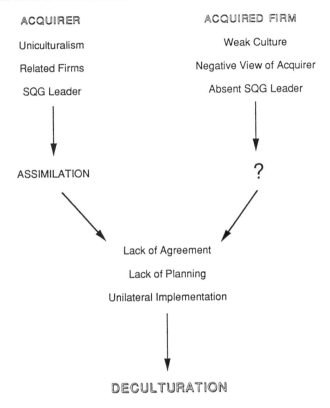

with their own operations. They wanted NTM to become part of them by losing its culture, identity, operational procedures, and so on. Such a mode was consistent with CS culture, strategy, leadership, and structure. Any firm it acquired was likely to be forced to adopt its culture and practices.

Choice of Acculturation for NTM. NTM employees never had the opportunity to make a choice regarding acculturation—a situation unfortunately very common, as most mergers are kept secret, and employees of one or both merger partners have no involvement in the determination of their own fate. The disappearance of Joe Anderson further added to the confusion, and their weak culture made them want to adopt another culture.

But their contact with CS made them realize that CS's culture was not one they would like to have replace their own, however weak their own might be. The absence of leadership to provide guidance and support rendered NTM's situation even less tenable. NTM employees were left, on the one hand, with a distintegrating culture and, on the other, with a new parent who unilaterally imposed an unwanted culture. These factors led to the destruction of their culture and generated the considerable resistance they showed toward adoption of their new parent's practices.

What Went Wrong

When faced with a case like the CS takeover of NTM, people's reactions usually fall into two groups. One group is likely to be appalled at how the merger was handled and at how CS's lack of sensitivity to cultural factors led to its own failure. People who have experienced a merger and its ensuing turnover and layoffs are likely to be part of that group, as are more long-term–oriented managers. Another, often highly vocal group will defend CS's actions and consider NTM's resistance professionally unacceptable. "After all, this *is* business," that latter group will say. "CS bought NTM, and it has the right to impose whatever procedures it wants." Both arguments have some merit, since neither of the merger partners achieved its goals, whether or not the goals were verbalized clearly.

Credit Services' Mistakes. As the organization that started the merger process and the one in control of the process, CS carried a major responsibility for the deculturation and the failure of the merger. Since CS's goal was not to liquidate NTM, but rather to grow into telemarketing, it did not achieve the goals of its merger. Its attempts at total assimilation of NTM fit its own strategy, culture, and leadership but failed to consider NTM's goals. Therefore, although the course of acculturation it had selected was appropriate, it was not agreed on and therefore was bound to fail.

CS's second error was the unilateral implementation of all changes. Once again, this approach fit well with CS culture and management style but not with the merger situation at hand. If NTM had been a willing partner, and if careful negotiations had been undertaken to discuss the changes, it may have been possible for NTM to accept CS's culture. There is no situation, however, even when there is agreement, when across-the-board unilateral actions are ever accepted; they always lead to resistance.

National Telemarketing's Mistakes. Much of what happened to NTM's employees was beyond their control. The destruction of their organization might have been avoided, 1,500 jobs saved, and countless stress-related problems averted had there been strong and competent leadership to negotiate the assimilation process. Since there was little interest in keeping NTM's culture, it would have been possible to ease the firm into a new culture. However, given the distinctive CS culture and its lack of fit with NTM's, such a melding may have been inappropriate. Strong leadership could have led NTM in the process of finding a suitable merger partner with an attractive culture.

SUMMARY

The factors that help avoid deculturation are:

- Agreement on the mode of acculturation
- Open communication
- Careful planning
- Monitoring of the merger process
- Presentation of the acquirer in a positive light
- Strengthening of the acquired firm's culture
- Avoidance of unilateral actions

The most important factor on the list is agreement on the mode of acculturation. The belief among many business executives and management
specialists is that if two cultures are similar, their merger is easier. Similarity, however, does not ensure success. For instance, two firms with very
strong authority-oriented cultures are each likely to hang on to their own
practices and be incapable of successful merger. In addition, similarity is
not necessary if the acquisition will be allowed to remain autonomous.

Agreement on the mode of acculturation is, however, essential. If the
two firms do not agree on how the merger will be implemented, they are
likely to move toward deculturation of the acquired firm.

Agreement on the mode of acculturation requires careful planning at
every stage. First, the choice of the merger partner has to fit the strategy
and culture of each firm, so detailed research is necessary regarding a
potential merger partner. Second, when a partner is found, extensive negotiation is required to reach an agreement not only on the mode of acculturation—which would determine the degree of contact—but also on
the manner and the speed at which the two firms will or will not be combined. Consequently, agreement on the mode has to be translated into
workable, specific agreements, and the plans for the merger and implementation process have to be monitored, reevaluated, and in many cases,
renegotiated for a period of time after the merger is consummated.
Whereas the planning process allows for agreement and joint—rather than
unilateral—actions by the merger partners, the monitoring process ensures
that agreements are executed properly.

The last factor essential in preventing deculturation is the avoidance of
any unilateral action. Mergers more often than not are between two firms
with unequal power. One firm takes over another. Many incorrectly assume
that the position of power that comes from the takeover entitles them to
impose their will on the "weaker" partner. Although it is both common
and possible, as well as legal, to do so, it is by no means wise for long-
term profitability. Unilateral action is likely to lead the human resources

of the acquired firm, one of its most valuable assets, to resist the merger and eventually leave the firm, thereby defeating the purpose of the merger.

Aside from all the strategic and cultural factors that lead to deculturation, the underlying cause of deculturation is *abuse* of power. Even if the merger does not begin with an agreement, it may not necessarily lead to deculturation if the acquirer does not decide to impose its will on the acquisition.

11

Conclusion: Summary and a Look at the Future

The major thesis of this book has been that in order to be successful a merger has to take into consideration the cultural and human factors involved in the merger, and both firms must be willing to take all the steps necessary for its implementation. The majority of mergers undertaken ignore cultural factors and instead focus on financial and operational issues. Most acquirers mistakenly assume that the only way two organizations can be combined is for one to become an integral and unrecognizable part of the other. Total assimilation is by no means the best or the only way two organizations can merge. Forcing assimilation regardless of the cultural, strategic, and organizational factors leads to strong resistance on the part of the acquired firm and delays any benefits of the merger for years.

THE COST OF RESISTANCE

Fear of Job Loss

One of the most common reasons for resistance is the fear of job loss. So many employees have witnessed the massive layoffs that follow mergers that their fear of job loss is ever present, regardless of all the promises made by the acquiring firm. Reliance on past events and accounts of other mergers create tremendous uncertainty about job security, even if the acquirer has no intention of firing any employees. And it is sometimes true that a merger becomes an excuse to implement labor reduction plans that were devised prior to the merger. But the potential, real or imagined, for job loss becomes a major focus of employees' attention during merger and leads them to resist any action related to its implementation.

Loss of Culture

Another, less tangible factor that leads to resistance is a sense that the culture of the acquired firm is being destroyed. As a result, employees experience a sense of loss, and all the financial and operational planning does not compensate them for such loss. Any change in the culture is perceived to be the end of the organization's identity and independence.

Many of the acquirer's decisions may be misperceived as attacks on the acquired firm's separate identity. For example, a needed technical change in the data base becomes the symbol of the parent company's interference. The intention of the parent may not have been to interfere, and the change may have been both needed and positive; however, the perception of the employees of the acquired firm is highly negative.

Dysfunctional Behaviors

The threat to job security and the sense of cultural loss lead employees of acquired firms to make decisions and undertake actions that are sometimes irrational. In some cases, these actions contribute to the destruction of the acquired organization. Employees sabotage their work, they do not come to work, and they resist the changes imposed by the new parent company.

One of the prevalent consequences of mergers is the time employees spend worrying about rumors and hunting for information. Even in those rare cases in which information is shared, many rumors will get started, and employees may spend more time worrying than working.

The stress created by the threat of job loss and the perceived or real loss of culture leads to considerable loss of productivity. Employees of acquired firms frequently report a large number of psychosomatic and stress-related problems. After a merger, the incidence of headaches and ulcers goes up. Backaches and accidents occur more often, and employees experience more coronary problems. They call in sick more often. In some cases, the stress caused by uncertainty and fear of job loss can even be fatal. These factors not only carry a tremendous cost—human and financial—for the corporation, but they also affect the employees' families and communities.

Effect on Outside Constituents

The lack of productivity that frequently results from a merger can affect immediate profits and the success of the merger. Often, the problem may become more serious as disgruntled employees communicate their lack of faith to outside constituents, thereby driving them away. Customers and suppliers are typically concerned about the merger of a firm they deal with.

They also experience uncertainty as they await changes or, in some cases, the total disappearance of a firm they have dealt with in the past. A supplier may lose a newly merged client when the new parent company either provides some of the supplies—as might be the case in vertical mergers—or contracts with new suppliers. The parent firm may also decide to close its acquired unit or move it to another location.

All these factors provide outside constituents with legitimate reasons for worrying. The reactions of the acquired firm's employees and managers to the merger become a key factor in managing the perceptions of outside constituents. The outsiders' fears can be alleviated when the employees express optimism and confidence, or they can be accentuated when employees of the acquired unit communicate their lack of faith in the merger to the customers. The lack of confidence can be conveyed passively by claiming ignorance of, and remaining unconcerned with, the outsiders' problems and worries. Disgruntled employees can also actively express their doubts and frustrations to clients and suppliers, thereby confirming their concerns.

The uncertainty and upheaval that result from mergers create feelings of loss and fear that affect the health and productivity of employees and the confidence of outside constituents. Fears and worries can be eased by actively planning and managing the human and cultural aspects of mergers.

TYPICAL ACTIONS

Ignoring the Problem

One of the most common ways of dealing with the fears and ensuing resistance of an acquired firm's employees is to ignore the problem. For different reasons, this is done by managers of both the acquiring and the acquired firms. Probably the most simple explanation for both groups' ignoring resistance is both lack of sensitivity to cultural issues and lack of experience in dealing with them. This factor not withstanding, the acquirer may ignore the resistance and fears employees face in the acquired unit because they appear unjustified since no change is planned. The acquirer erroneously assumes that employees of the acquiring firm will come to see that nothing major is changing, and consequently, their resistance will simply go away.

Another reason an acquirer may ignore concerns and resistance is because they are actually legitimate: Perhaps there are plans for large-scale changes and layoffs, and inevitably both jobs and culture will be lost as a result. However, if the acquiring firm is not yet ready to announce such plans, it will remain silent. While the acquirer may have legitimate reasons for its silence, the human cost is often very high. Regardless of the reasons for silence and the acquiring firm's unwillingness to deal with the concerns of the employees of the acquired firm, the result is that the employees continue to worry and in many cases, the ongoing silence further fuels their uneasiness, rendering them even less productive.

Managers of an acquired firm try to ignore resistance for other reasons. In the most straightforward case, they are so busy with the transition process that they simply do not have time to share information. In other cases, they are as apprehensive and resentful as their employees, but they have neither the information nor the tools nor the power to help. In addition, while many managers express a desire to communicate with their employees, they are afraid of losing their trust if the information they provide in good faith is later found to be inaccurate, so they often report a sense of frustration and helplessness as they choose to remain silent and hope that the situation will resolve itself. Finally, the managers of the acquired firm, like their counterparts in the acquiring firm, may have ulterior motives for ignoring their employees' anxieties; they know that their employees' concerns are valid but they do not want to share information with them because they know the information may have negative impact.

Regardless of the reasons for ignoring employee apprehension and resistance, this course of action is likely to be ineffective and, in many cases, will aggravate the situation. Employees interpret the silence as a sign of trouble and make plans to leave, and not knowing what is going on and not having any means of obtaining information only increase the uncertainty. Consequently, the rumor mills become highly active, often even the center of all the employees' energy. Therefore, although very common, ignoring employee concerns is an ineffective way to manage the merger process.

Forced Turnover

Another way to deal with employee resistance and restlessness in mergers is to eliminate those who are resisting, through a variety of means—for example, simple cuts in jobs or drastic changes in job descriptions and responsibility intended to cause "voluntary" turnover. In addition, many companies also make heavy use of early retirement packages. All these actions lead to the massive turnover typically associated with mergers.

Part of the decision to cut jobs is based on sound, long-term business planning motivated by strategic plans for cost cutting or achievement of synergy between the two merged organizations. However, another part of the push to drive out employees of the acquired firm is related to the desire to have a fresh start, and those who do not fit with the culture of the new parent are forced to leave. The departure of those employees may frequently ease and shorten the implementation of the parent's requests in the short run. However, by losing the human resources of the firm it has acquired—however few—an acquirer destroys one of the essential components that made the target firm attractive and successful in the first place. Additionally, the best employees are the ones most likely to leave first, further delaying any possible benefits from the merger. Consequently, although the turnover strategy is attractive in the short run, in the long run, the experience that is lost—along with the costs of replacing those employees—becomes a major obstacle to the merger's success.

Ethical Dilemma

We have heard many managers explain why communication lapse and layoffs are necessary. They express a need to cut costs in order to survive and profit in a competitive industry. Informing employees of upcoming layoffs, they believe, will make them angry and lead to irrational and potentially dangerous behavior. Managers also worry that the best people will "jump ship," and they want to be in control of who stays and who goes. And many managers have voiced the opinion that, as managers, they have the right to make decisions in confidence and no obligation to share information with their employees. Although all these explanations are used frequently and they all may appear to have some legitimacy, they are difficult to support for two very different reasons. First, from an ethical point of view, employees have the right to be given sufficient notice concerning job changes and/or job loss. Second, all employees deserve to be treated with dignity and respect. Ethical and humane perspectives are all too often lacking at the height of merger mania and in the pursuit of short-term profit.

One recently acquired organization saw its 2,000 person work force reduced to only 400 in a matter of eighteen months. Every day, employees simply waited to hear new names called out. Those who were called left to meet with personnel and returned half an hour later, accompanied by security officers carrying boxes. They packed their offices or desks and were escorted out of the building, never to return. While severance packages were often generous, they in no way compensated employees for the stress and embarrassment they suffered. Those remaining literally stopped working and constantly worried about their own jobs; in addition, they developed resentment and disdain for their own and the parent company's managers.

Unfortunately, cases such as this one are not the exception. From both ethical and humane points of view, withholding information from employees and executing poorly planned layoffs are unacceptable, and from a practical point of view, neither tactic is functional. When information is not shared, rumors abound, creating resistance, fear, and often irrational behavior. Layoffs are suspected, and whether or not they occur and whether or not they are announced, their looming potential seriously affects productivity and merger success.

RECOMMENDED ACTIONS

The majority of mergers undertaken rely on (1) ignoring problems and (2) forced turnover to deal with the cultural aspects of combining two firms. The choice of these approaches is often made by default, because managers are not well trained to deal with the "softer" aspects of management. In addition, the short-term–profit orientation often makes these two strategies attractive and renders more long-term approaches too complicated. However, in order to gain long-term success and profitability from a merger, cultural factors have to be dealt with and many other strategies have to be considered.

Good-Faith Negotiation

A merger implementation needs to involve the process of good-faith negotiation. The two merger partners have to come together to discuss the upcoming changes in all areas and to consider the effects that those changes might have on employee jobs and the cultures of the two organizations. Although the acquired firm is usually the one most affected, it is important also to consider the way in which the acquiring firm will change as a result of the merger. A key factor in the negotiation over cultural impact is awareness of the available options and the preferences of the parties involved.

Awareness of Strategy and Culture. The modes of acculturation presented earlier provide the cornerstone for negotiation discussions. To clearly articulate its motives and goals for a merger, the acquirer must be aware of its preference for the mode of acculturation. What does it want from this merger? Why is it targeting this particular firm? In what ways, if at all, will this firm complement the existing operation?

In addition to its strategic goals, an acquirer has to come to the negotiating table aware of its culture. In particular, how tolerant is the culture? Is there strong pressure to standardize all activities, or are there openness and flexibility regarding operations and management styles? The answers to these questions indicate the extent to which the new acquisition will be expected to comply with the parent firm. Another good indicator of the way in which the new acquisition will be managed is the way past acquisitions have been administered.

Overall, acquirers have to be aware of their strategy and culture before selecting merger as a strategy. It is only through this awareness that an acquirer can come to negotiate with its target and plan for the process of merger implementation.

Awareness of Cultural Strength and Image of Acquirer. The managers of an acquired firm have the heavy burden of fighting for their organization in a situation where they often have limited power. So it is essential for them to know how strong the culture of their organization is. Will employees resist the parent company? Do they want to preserve their culture? What are the factors and changes that are most likely to be resisted? What are the assumptions that are closely held? Which ones will be easier to give up? This knowledge is invaluable in negotiating with the parent company concerning the extent to which the acquired firm is willing to change and preparing for resistance in other areas.

Before negotiations, managers of the acquired firm also need to determine the way in which the acquirer is perceived. Is its image positive? Is it seen as a successful, respectable company? Are employees at least partly interested in some of what the partner may have to offer? Which aspects of the acquirer's organization are most likely to be accepted by employees? These factors, along with the strength of its own culture, will provide the acquired firm's managers with a direction for negotiation over cultural change.

Agreeing on a Mode of Acculturation. Once the two merger partners have information that allows them to determine the mode of acculturation most acceptable to each of them, they need to reach an agreement acceptable to *both* of them. It is essential to remember that there is no need for the two organizations to be similar as long as they can agree on how the merger will be implemented. If there is no immediate concensus, the process of reaching an agreement over acculturation is likely to be difficult and lengthy, particularly given the unequal status of the two merger partners. As the more powerful party, the acquirer may have a tendency to cut negotiations short and simply dictate, "We are buying you; you do it *our* way," leaving no options for the acquired unit. As mentioned earlier, although this approach may get short-term results, it guarantees resistance and long-term problems and losses.

The difficulty encountered in resolving the differences over acculturation preferences will depend on where each party stands. As presented in Chapter 5 (see Figure 5.5), if the two parties are diagonally opposed, agreement will be very difficult to achieve. For example, if one partner is considering assimilation while the other is looking for separation, it is much easier to move both of them toward integration than to get either to agree with the other. Of course, the choice of acculturation has to be consistent with strategy and culture. An acquired firm that may be looking for separation from its parent company may change its preference if it can be convinced of the value of the parent company's culture. The acquirer can focus on highlighting its success and on demonstrating how some of its practices can be beneficial to its new acquisition.

It is essential to negotiate the acculturation process in good faith in much the same way that other aspects of the merger are negotiated. Once agree-

ment over the mode of acculturation is reached, the process of implementation has to be planned out carefully.

Plans for Implementation and Monitoring the Process

Premerger planning and negotiations have to be followed by postmerger
implementation of the various agreements. Many plans may require renegotiation as the two partners find new ways to cooperate or decide to
end some collaborative projects. Regardless of which mode is finally selected, the course of acculturation has to be monitored and steered back
on course whenever necessary. For example, employees of an acquirer may
have difficulty allowing the new acquisition to be independent in spite of
all the premerger agreements for separation. Unless the executives and
managers of both firms are monitoring the process, there will be no way
for them to correct the problem quickly and keep the merger on course.

In other situations, the choices for acculturation may change as contact
between the two firms increases. Although increased contact typically leads
to higher conflict, members of one or both organizations may also find
new, attractive features of the merger partner that they may want to em-
ulate in their own organization, so interaction may lead to a renegotiation
of, and a new agreement on, the course of acculturation. Such a process
is eased by monitoring the way in which the two firms are combining their
operations and people.

Communication

One of the key elements in managing the process of combining two
organizations is maintaining open lines of communication. As mentioned
earlier, the tendency not to share information is often encouraged either
by the lack of clear information or by a desire to avoid giving bad news.
Contrary to this tendency, there is considerable research that suggests that
open communication and sharing of information constitute one of the best
ways to help reduce the stress and anxiety that result from mergers. It is
the responsibility of the executives and managers of both firms to provide
employees with clear information. In most cases, technical data are communicated; for example, many firms will provide information about changes
in benefits packages. In spite of its complexity, the information is concrete
and easy to convey, so it is communicated to employees.

Other, less concrete information is often left out, frequently because
managers themselves do not have all the facts. It is imperative that employees receive that exact message: They need to know precisely what the
manager does and does not know. This knowledge reduces uncertainty
and develops trust in management. Pretending to have all the answers and
refusing to provide information are risky strategies that should be avoided.

A variety of mechanisms can be created to provide employees with answers to their many questions. For example, official newsletters and merger progress reports can be distributed on a regular basis. Certain managers can be kept up to date on all the merger negotiations and implementation plans, and they would, in turn, be designated as information centers whom employees would be encouraged to contact with questions. Information hot lines could be created, and regular presentations could be set up. The goal of all these mechanisms is to reduce the amount of uncertainty and stress by defusing rumors and increasing the flow of factual and accurate information.

Managing Perceptions. One aspect of an effective communication plan is to manage employee and manager perception in both organizations. In particular, the acquirer has to be careful that its actions and decisions are accurate reflections of its intentions. For instance, a new parent company's inquiry about a certain operating system may be perceived by employees of the acquired organization as an intention to reduce their independence. In such a situation, regardless of its accuracy, the goal of inquiry becomes almost irrelevant, whereas the perception of the employees of the acquired firm becomes the most important factor.

Mergers as Partnerships, Not Power Struggles

The main purpose of a merger is to increase the profitability and influence of the newly formed organization. Two organizations combined are stronger than each alone. They either complement each other, or they duplicate each other and together are stronger. Two combined organizations have the potential to achieve goals both more efficiently and effectively, and their strength should allow them better strategic positioning in their industry and in national and international markets. A merger is meant to be a strategic move, it is supposed to create a partnership.

Very few of the mergers that have taken place in the past few years seem to have been undertaken for any of these reasons. Even if the initial goals were strategic and focused on long-term success and profitability, the focus seems to have quickly shifted to a power struggle. So many mergers have been about power, as stronger organizations attempt to dominate weaker ones. They impose their cultures and systems not because they are the most strategically sound but because they have the power to do so. As a result, a merger becomes a power struggle rather than a sound business decision. And while a power struggle may be appropriate when dealing with a competitor, this kind of sparring is inappropriate when two organizations are attempting to join forces so that together they can become more competitive.

As long as the focus of a merger is on dominating the partner rather than on forging cooperation and collaboration, it is unlikely to live up to early predictions for success. Power struggles alienate employees and managers and strip one or both organizations of their most valuable resource: its people and their commitment to performance.

A LOOK AT THE FUTURE

The mergers of the 1970s and the 1980s have not been overwhelmingly successful. Hostile takeovers and proxy battles have forced many firms into debt and pushed their managers into short-term thinking to protect themselves from becoming a takeover target. Unsuccessful mergers and hostile takeovers have had direct and indirect negative effects on the U.S. economy at a time when many foreign competitors are increasing their hold on world markets.

What is needed for the 1990s and beyond is to rediscover mergers as a strategic alliance and as a partnership rather than as a war. Many firms can, and should, benefit from consolidation of their business with other firms. However, the benefits from merger cannot be realized in a hostile internal environment. Mergers have to provide opportunities for cooperation and collaboration, for it is only then that the much-sought-after synergies can be fully achieved. Therefore, merger success in the years to come relies heavily on being able to maintain that atmosphere of cooperation. This factor makes the understanding of cultural processes even more essential. A CEO undertaking a merger must possess the skills to negotiate the acculturation process.

Global Mergers

The continued globalization of world markets, the possibility of a united Europe, the developing strength of the Association of South East Asian Nations (ASEAN), and the signing of the North American Free Trade Agreement between the United States, Canada, and Mexico all create new opportunities for mergers. These new mergers would be between firms in different countries not only with different organizational cultures but also with different societal cultures. Forging alliances across national and cultural boundaries brings to the forefront the vital necessity of recognizing and managing cultural differences and the acculturation process not only within organizations but also across cultures.

Bibliography

Alluto, J. A., & Hrebiniak, L. G. (1975). *Research on commitment to employing organization: Preliminary findings on a study of managers graduation from engineering and MBA programs.* Paper presented at the National Academy of Management, New Orleans.

Anderson, C. R., Hellriegel, D., & Slocum, J. W. (1977). Managerial response to environmentally induced stress. *Academy of Management Journal*, 20(2), 260–272.

Ansoff, H. I. (1965). *Corporate strategy: An analytic approach to business policy for growth and expansion.* New York: McGraw-Hill.

Argyris, C., & Schon, D. A. (1978). *Organizational learning.* Reading, MA: Addison-Wesley.

Berry, J. W. (1980). Social and cultural change. In H. C. Triandis & R. W. Brislin (Eds.), *Handbook of cross-cultural psychology* (Vol. 5, pp. 211–279). Boston: Allyn & Bacon.

————. (1983). Acculturation: A comparative analysis of alternative forms. In R. J. Samuda & S. L. Woods (Eds.), *Perspectives in immigrant and minority education* (pp. 11–270). Orlando, FL: Academic Press.

Berry, J. W., & Annis, R. C. (1974). Acculturative stress: The role of ecology, culture and differentiation. *Journal of Cross-Cultural Psychology*, 5, 382–406.

Buono, A. F., & Bowditch, J. L. (1989). *The human side of mergers and acquisitions.* San Francisco: Jossey-Bass.

Corporate culture (1980, October 27). *Business Week*, pp. 148–160.

Deal, T. E., & Kennedy, A. A. (1982). *Corporate cultures: The rites and rituals of corporate life.* Reading, MA: Addison-Wesley.

Dumaine, B. (1990, January 29). Corporate citizenship. *Fortune*, pp. 50, 54.

Evans, G. (1991, February). Denmark: Pinstripes versus the Trinity. *Euromoney*, pp. 63–66.

Galbraith, J. R. (1983). Strategy and organization planning. *Human Resource Management*, *22* (1/2), 64–77.

Gaughan, P. (1991). *Mergers and acquisitions*. New York: Harper Collins.

Gupta, A. K. (1988). Contingency perspectives on strategic leadership: Current knowledge and future research directions. In D. C. Hambrick (Ed.), *The executive effect: Concepts and methods for studying top managers* (pp. 141–178). Greenwich, CT: JAI Press.

Hall, R. H. (1977). *Organizations: Structures, processes, and outcomes*. 2nd ed. Englewood Cliffs, NJ: Prentice-Hall.

Hambrick, D. C., & Mason, P. A. (1984). Upper echelon: The organization as a reflection of its top management. *Academy of Management Review*, *9*, 193–206.

Harrigan, K. R. (1983). *Strategies for vertical integration*. Lexington, MA: Lexington Books.

Haspeslagh, P. C., & Jemison, D. B. (1991). *Managing acquisitions: Creating value through corporate renewal*. New York: Free Press.

Kerr, S., & Jermier, J. M. (1978). Substitutes for leadership: Their meaning and measurement. *Organizational Behavior and Human Performance*, *22*, 395–403.

Kester, W. C. (1991). *Japanese takeover*. Boston: Harvard University Press.

Kotin, J., & Sharaf, M. (1976). Management succession and administrative style. *Psychiatry*, *30*, 237–248.

Labich, K. (1988, January 18). Big changes at Big Brown. *Fortune*, p. 56.

Larson, E. (1988, July). Forever young. *Inc.*, pp. 50–56.

Malekzadeh, A. R., & Nahavandi, A. (1990, May/June). Making mergers work by managing the cultures. *Journal of Business Strategy*, pp. 55–57.

Manz, C. C., & Sims, H. P. (1987, March). Leading workers to lead themselves: The external leadership of self-managing work teams. *Administrative Science Quarterly*, pp. 106–129.

Miller, D. (1987). The genesis of configuration. *Academy of Management Review*, *12*, 686–701.

Miller, D., Kets De Vries, M.F.R., & Toulouse, J. M. (1982). Top executive locus of control and its relationship to strategy-making, structure, and environment. *Academy of Management Journal*, *25*(2), 237–253.

Nahavandi, A., & Malekzadeh, A. R. (1988). Acculturation in mergers and acquisitions. *Academy of Management Review*, *13*(1), 79–90.

———. (1993). Leader style in strategy and organizational performance: An integrative framework. *Journal of Management Studies*, *30*, pp. 405–425.

O'Reilly, C. (1989, Summer). Corporations, culture, and commitment: Motivation and social control in organizations. *California Management Review*, *31*, 9–25.

Personnel Administrator (1989, August), pp. 84–90.

Pfeffer, J. (1983). Organizational demography. In L. L. Cummings & B. W. Staw (Eds.), *Research in organizational behavior* (pp. 299–357). Greenwich, CT: JAI Press.

Picker, I., Shapiro, H. D., VonWyss, G., Conger, L., & Karp, R. (1991). Mergers and acquisitions: Strategic is the word. *Institutional Investor*, *25*(1), 74–81.

Porter, M. E. (1980). *Competitive strategy*. NY: Free Press.

Rumelt, R. P. (1974). *Strategy, structure, and economic performance*. Boston, MA: Harvard Business School Press.

Sathe, V. (1985). *Culture and related corporate realities*. Homewood, IL: Irwin.

Schein, E. H. (1985). *Organizational culture and leadership*. San Francisco: Jossey-Bass.

Schweiger, D. M., & DeNisi, A. S. (1991). Communication with employees following a merger: A longitudinal field experiment. *Academy of Management Journal, 34*(1), 110–135.

Singh, H., & Harianto, F. (1989). Management-board relationships, takeover risk, and the adoption of golden parachutes. *Academy of Management Journal, 32*(1), 7–24.

Song, J. H. (1982). Diversification strategies and the experience of top executives of large firms. *Strategic Management Journal, 3*, 377–380.

Walsh, J. P. (1988). Top management turnover following mergers and acquisitions. *Strategic Management Journal, 9*, 173–183.

———. (1989). Doing a deal: Merger and acquisition negotiations and their impact upon target company top management turnover. *Strategic Management Journal, 10*, 307–322.

Walter, G. M. (1985). Culture collision in mergers and acquisitions. In P. J. Frost, L. F. Moore, M. R. Louis, C. C. Lundberg, & J. Martin (Eds.), *Organizational culture* (pp. 301–314). Beverly Hills, CA: Sage.

Whiting, R. (1991, February). Material Research gets a new lease on life. *Electronic Business, 4*, 34–36.

Index

About the Authors

AFSANEH NAHAVANDI is Associate Professor of management at Arizona State University West. Her articles about mergers and leadership have been published in the *Journal of Management Studies*, the *Academy of Management Review*, the *Journal of Business Strategy*, the *Canadian Journal of Administrative Sciences*, and *Group and Organization Studies*.

ALI R. MALEKZADEH is Associate Professor of strategic management at Arizona State University West. His articles about mergers and the strategic management of technology have been published in the *Journal of Management Studies*, the *Academy of Management Review*, the *Journal of Business Strategy*, and the *Academy of Management Best Paper Proceedings*.